FOIE GRAS AND TRUMPETS

The 'Gondola dinner party' given in 1905 at the Savoy Hotel by the millionaire George A. Kessler in honour of the birthday of King Edward VII

FOIE GRAS
AND
TRUMPETS

CHARLES NEILSON GATTEY

WITH A FOREWORD BY
KIRI TE KANAWA

CONSTABLE · LONDON

First published in Great Britain 1984
by Constable and Company Limited
10 Orange Street, London WC2H 7EG
Copyright © Charles Neilson Gattey 1984
ISBN 0 09 465840 4
Set in Linotron Plantin 11pt by
Rowland Phototypesetting Ltd,
Bury St Edmunds, Suffolk
Printed in Great Britain by
St Edmundsbury Press,
Bury St Edmunds, Suffolk

To Ken Davison who suggested the title – from Sydney Smith's 'My idea of heaven is, eating pâtés de foie gras to the sound of trumpets.'

That convivial clergyman would have approved of a foie-gras-loving cousin of the Duke of Bedford, whose ashes, in deference to his wishes, lie in a foie-gras jar in the family chapel at Chenies awaiting the angels sounding their trumpets.

Contents

[9]

Contents

PART II

Illustrations

Foreword
by Kiri Te Kanawa

It gives me very great pleasure to welcome this extremely enjoyable book. As its author points out, most singers like to eat and drink well, and I am certainly no exception. After all, we use up so much energy singing on stage that we are bound to feel hungry afterwards. But much as I enjoy sumptuous meals in the world's great restaurants, it is home cooking that I still like best – meals that I have prepared myself and can eat with my family. So I am particularly honoured that the distinguished chef, Monsieur Anton Mosimann, should have created a recipe and named it after me. I much look forward to making *Crêpe sans rival à la Kiri Te Kanawa*: it will present a decisive challenge to my cooking ability, and will make an exciting change from my present favourite dessert of Kiwi fruit Pavlova.

PART
I

Beware!

Maria Callas at one time weighed some 97 kilos. When Sir Rudolf Bing engaged her to sing at the Met, it was on the understanding that she should become much slimmer. Through a diet mainly of lettuce leaves, she achieved this, and made her brilliant début in New York in October 1956. Her close friend Marlene Dietrich feared that the loss of weight might have weakened her, and, becoming anxious during the rehearsals, spent several hours boiling down eight pounds of the best beef to a quart of the very finest broth.

'It's wonderful!' Maria declared. 'How kind! Do tell me – what brand of beef cubes did you use?'

So, reader, if you spend time and money preparing gourmet dishes, please be sure that your guests would not prefer corned beef hash. As M. Fayot observed to Jules Janin, the French dramatic critic: 'It is difficult to write well, but it is a hundred times more difficult to know how to dine well.' And, as that eminent gastronome André L. Simon, has written: 'All good cooks, like all great artists, must have an audience worth cooking for or singing to.'

 # Apéritif-Prélude

From ancient times, people have found that music has added to the enjoyment of eating food and has helped its digestion. Sturgeons, lampreys, and mullets would be ushered in at Roman banquets to the strains of flute and lyre. In the Elizabethan age, we find Sir Francis Drake's chaplain describing how on a voyage he had not 'omitted to make provision also for ornament and delight, carrying with him for this purpose expert musicians,' while a Spanish captain taken prisoner at that time wrote that he dined and supped to the music of viols. Deloney, a novelist of the same period, says of his character, Tom Dove, a clothier, 'It was as sure as an Act of Parliament that he could not digest his meat without musick.'

In King James I's reign, the London Musicians' Company warned its members in 1606 that they would be fined 3s 4d if they agreed to be employed at banquets where the performers numbered less than four. In view of the Puritans' insistence on plain living, it is surprising to learn from contemporary accounts that music was usually played continually when Oliver Cromwell had guests, as if he were royalty. That music-lover

Samuel Pepys, when entertained to dinner at the Dolphin, complained, 'I expected musique, the missing of which spoiled my dinner.' On a later occasion therefore, dining at the same inn with the Commissioner of Ordnance, he took steps to ensure that he was not deprived of it again and recorded with satisfaction: 'Good musick at my direction.'

We learn from Pepys's *Diaries* that one could hire 'freecooks' to prepare meals for special occasions, as he did once for a company dinner of 'stewed carp, roasted chicken, a Jowle of Salmon, neat's tongue, a tansy and cheese'. They were 'merry all the afternoon, talking, singing, and piping on the flageolet'.

When the future United States were first colonized, its settlers were often deprived of the frills of life, but music at meals was regarded by some as a necessity. Judge Sewall of Boston grumbled in his journal that at a Council dinner there he had 'no musick, though the Lieutenant Governor had promised it'. Describing a visit to England in 1689, he mentions with pleasure how at an inn in Cambridge, while he and friends 'had a Legg Mutton boiled and Colly-Flowers, Carrots, Roasted Fowls, and a dish of Pease', three musicians entered with 'two Harps and a Violin, and gave us musick'.

Most celebrated chefs have been music-lovers, as was the Duke of Abercorn's chef in the last century. He had previously been employed by the Duke of Richmond and had refused to accompany him to Ireland at a salary of £400 a year on learning that there was no Italian opera in Dublin.

Abraham Hayward in his delightful book on *The Art of Dining*, published in 1899, wrote: 'The present Duke of Beaufort had a Neapolitan confectioner who was thoroughly impressed with the dignity, and imbued with the spirit, of his art. His Grace was one night in bed and fast asleep, when he was roused by a knock at his door, which was impatiently repeated. He asked who was there. "It is only me, Signor Duca. I was at the opera, and I have been dreaming of the music. It was Donizetti's, and I have an idea. I have this instant invented a sorbet. I have named it after that divine composer, and I hastened to inform your Grace."'

—————————— ★ ——————————
The gastronome saved by music
—————————— ★ ——————————

In 1825, two months before he died at the age of seventy, a French lawyer, a cousin of Mme Récamier, published what is still commonly regarded as the greatest book on gastronomy, *La Physiologie du Goût*, a stimulating guide to the art of living which had taken him many years to write. It is witty and anecdotal, also instructive, and it advances some ingenious and controversial theories. Narrowly escaping the guillotine during the French Revolution, its author, Jean Anthelme Brillat-Savarin, fled to New York where, being a brilliant musician, he found employment as a violinist in a theatre orchestra. Returning later to Paris, he became Conseiller à la Cour de Cassation, where he was admired for his legal skill and imposing presence.

Brillat-Savarin owed his life to music. When the Reign of Terror was raging, he rode on his horse, La Joie, to Dôle and there applied to a Revolutionary Tribunal Commissioner named Prôt for a safe conduct, to avoid prison. When this official's wife learnt that Brillat-Savarin, like herself, loved music and had a trained voice, she invited him to supper. 'Mme Prôt sang, I sang, we sang; never did I sing so feelingly,' the lawyer relates. 'Her husband wanted to go to bed, but she would not hear of it until we ended with a duet which rang out like the challenge of a bugle call. When we said good-night, she whispered to me that I should have what I wanted. She would see to that. Next morning I had my safe conduct. I went home with my head high on my shoulders and thanks to Harmony, that beloved daughter of Heaven, my ascension thither was postponed for a number of years.'

Women who are so fond of food that they would rather be overweight than curb their appetites will find much comfort in Brillat-Savarin's book:

Gourmandise is by no means unbecoming in women; it agrees with the delicacy of their organs, and serves to compensate them for some pleasures from which they are obliged to abstain, and for some evils to which Nature appears to have condemned them. Nothing is more pleasant to see than a pretty *gourmande* in action . . . she is irresistible. . . .

Gourmandise is favourable to beauty. . . . It gives more brilliancy to the eyes, more freshness to the skin, more support to the muscles; and as it is certain in physiology that it is the depression of the muscles which causes wrinkles . . . it is equally true to say that those who understand eating are comparatively ten years younger than those who are strangers to this science. Painters and sculptors are well aware of this, for they always portray those who deliberately starve themselves, such as misers and hermits, as sunken-cheeked, furrow-browed, scraggy-necked, deathly pale, and altogether decrepit.

Again, *gourmandise* makes for happy marriage. Husband and wife sharing this interest have the most agreeable reason for meeting at meal times . . . a common want summons the pair to table and retains them there as long as possible.

Brillat-Savarin comments further on those unable to appreciate fine food:

There are individuals to whom Nature has denied a refinement of organs, or a continuity of attention, without which the most succulent dishes pass unobserved. Physiology has proved that some unfortunates have tongues poorly provided with nerves for detecting subtle differences in flavours. Such persons react to objects of taste like the blind do to light. The other unfortunates consist of those who pay no attention to what they are eating, chatterboxes, business men, the ambitious, all those who seek to occupy themselves with two things at once and eat only to be filled. Such a person was Napoleon, who was irregular in his meals and ate fast and carelessly. As a result, he lost the Battles of Borodino and Leipzig.

The gourmet was considered by Brillat-Savarin to be superior to the orator. "All men use their tongues for speaking, but very few for tasting.'

It was customary during Brillat-Savarin's lifetime for banquets to last several hours and for hundreds of dishes to be served. So it is not surprising that he should have written: 'A banquet is probably the most fatiguing thing in the world, except ditch-digging. It is the insanest of all recreations. The inventor of it overlooked no detail that could cause weariness, distress, harassment, and acute and long-sustained misery of mind and body.'

The conclusions which Brillat-Savarin reached in his work were, he maintained, based on careful observation. 'Tell me what you eat and I will tell you what you are,' he says. He gives much practical advice such as, 'To make good soup, the pot must simmer,' and advice on detecting from people's physiognomy whether they were worthy of being invited to partake of gourmet cooking. 'Those predisposed to epicurism are for the most part of middling height, broad-faced, bright-eyed, with small foreheads, short noses, fleshy lips and rounded chins. They make agreeable guests, accept all that is offered them, eat without hurry, and taste with discrimination . . . Those, on the contrary, to whom nature has denied an aptitude for the enjoyment of taste, are long-faced, long-nosed, and long-eyed: whatever their stature, they have something lanky about them. They have dark, lanky hair, and are never in good condition. It was one of them who invented trousers.' Clearly, the author considered sansculotterie one of the worst excesses of the French Revolution.

Brillat-Savarin had a sister who was also a gourmet and who outlived him. Her end would have pleased him for she died on her hundredth birthday after enjoying a delightful dinner and calling loudly for more dessert.

★
Haute cuisine
★

A dinner that was *haute cuisine* in both senses of the phrase took place in the auditorium of the second Covent Garden Theatre in 1820. It was given by John Ambrose West (1786–1868), a most enterprising engineer and originator of a great many of the gasworks in various parts of England. He installed gas to light London's Guildhall, and when there was a serious risk of an explosion he climbed on top of the hall to cut off a pipe. Then his foot slipped and he fell: had he not landed on a parapet, West would have been killed. Next, he changed the system of illumination from flares to gas at Drury Lane, and then at Covent Garden.

During the summer of 1820, when Covent Garden was closed for the recess so as to be completely redecorated, a superb, gas-fed, central chandelier was hung from the ceiling of the auditorium. This aroused much controversy, and to allay the fears of those who thought that the roof could not bear such a weight, West had a large platform erected on top of the chandelier where a dinner of several courses was served to himself and his guests without mishap before the theatre reopened on September 18 (with a performance of Shakespeare's *Romeo and Juliet*). The building was destroyed by fire in 1856, but the cut-glass and quartz of the chandelier were salvaged, reassembled, and suspended in the Crush Bar, where it still is.

★
Royal musical gourmets
★

King Edward VII loved fine food from his days as an under-graduate at Oxford, when Prince Albert complained in a letter that his son preferred eating to mental effort. He was extremely fond of game, one of his favourite dishes being *Côtelettes de bécassines à la Souvaroff*, which consisted of snipe, boned and halved, stuffed with foie gras and forcemeat, shaped into small cutlets and grilled in a pig's caul, served with small slices of truffle and Madeira sauce. In addition to his other meals, he often enjoyed as a bedtime snack grilled oysters washed down by champagne.

Crayfish cooked in Chablis was the dish that Queen Alexandra liked most. She had a passion for opera and during the season she never went less than once a week to Covent Garden. Gabriel Tschumi, the royal chef, described in his reminiscences how he catered for his employers' friends there. Early in the afternoon before the evening performance, hampers were packed with tablecloths, napkins, silver, precious gold plate, and all else that was needed to feed thirty or so guests. Six footmen would convey this to the Royal Opera House in the old horse-brake bearing the King's arms. Tschumi would accompany them, together with a dozen or more additional hampers containing the fare to be served at supper, the menu for which had been approved a day earlier. Courses numbered between nine and a dozen, so, since each guest had a plate for each one, there were sometimes nearly 400 plates to be carried up to the room behind the Royal Box. At least the food was all served cold.

At about five o'clock Tschumi and his staff started setting out the supper, so as to give themselves ample time to fetch from Buckingham Palace anything that might have been overlooked. Cold consommé was always served first, and to finish with there were *pâtisseries* such as *petites pâtisseries fondantes* or *pâtisseries Parisiennes*, and a choice of three or four desserts made from strawberries or other fresh fruit. In between, the royal party would feast on lobster mayonnaise, cold trout, duck, lamb cutlets, plovers' eggs, chicken, tongue and ham jelly, and a variety of sandwiches.

Nellie Melba's lover, Philippe, Duc d'Orléans, kept a private suite at the Savoy Hotel, and one night when Edward VII, then Prince of Wales, joined them for dinner there, Escoffier prepared for the occasion a gastronomic novelty which he called *Cuisses de nymphes à l'aurore* – which some might have considered to be somewhat daring, since the affair of the heir to the throne and Lily Langtry had become the talk of the town. The Prince, however, was delighted with the dish and asked to be told the recipe. Escoffier revealed that the 'nymphs' thighs' were cold frogs' legs poached in a court-bouillon with Moselle wine, and then placed on a layer of champagne jelly with chervil and tarragon leaves between the legs to resemble grass. This was covered with more champagne jelly to look like water, and served with a fish sauce.

A far more daring dish was once set before the Prince in Paris. It was, in fact, brought to him on an enormous covered tray, and when the lid was raised there lay the celebrated courtesan, Cora Pearl, naked save for some sprigs of parsley and a string of pearls.

Diners have at times wondered after whom *Crêpes Suzette* were named. François Latry of the Savoy once gave his version of this event in a letter to *The Times*: 'Mlle Suzette was a member of the *Comédie-Française*. In 1837, acting the part of a chambermaid, she had to serve pancakes on the stage. They were prepared by the Restaurant Marivaux and the creator . . . was Joseph, who afterwards came to London as manager of the Savoy Restaurant. His original recipe was changed, complicated, but never surpassed. The secret of the dish is its unctuousness and its aroma, due to the mixture of the melted butter and the perfume of the orange, the only one that must be represented in the *Crêpes Suzette*.'

Contrary to the then general practice, Latry insisted that true *Crêpes Suzette* must not only have the sole flavour of orange but must never be set alight.

There is, however, another strong claimant to the title of creator of this popular delicacy. The celebrated chef, Henri Charpentier, in his memoirs, *Those Rich and Great Ones*, relates how in 1894 when he was only aged fourteen and was a *commis des rangs* at the *Café de Paris* in Monte Carlo, Edward, Prince of Wales, would lunch there regularly. Often young Henri helped

[27]

to carry in the dishes, and one day it fell to his lot to wait upon the Prince and his party of seven men and a young girl who was the daughter of one of them. The Prince asked whether there was anything special for luncheon, and Henri replied that there would be a sweet course never before served to anyone, which he himself had originated. He had often experimented making what were known as French pancakes, and had been trained by his foster-mother's eldest son, Jean Camous, chef of the Grand Hotel in Monte Carlo. His method with the wafer-thin *crêpes* was to fold them in four, like a lady's handkerchief, and to prepare a sauce made by blending equal quantities of maraschino, curaçao and kirsch with melted butter and flavouring this mixture with orange- and lemon-flavoured sugar. As he worked in the kitchen of the Café de Paris intent on pleasing the Prince of Wales, Charpentier writes that he had not yet perfected the recipe and was taken by surprise when the liqueurs in the chafing-dish caught fire. Had he ruined the pancakes and would he be sacked, he wondered?

He tasted the syrup, and fear turned to joy. It was, he thought, 'the most delicious melody of sweet flavours' he had ever sipped. The accidental conflagration had proved to be just what was required to attain perfection. As if inspired, he recalls, he plunged the folded pancakes into the boiling sauce, submerged them, turned them adroitly. 'And then, again inspired, I added two more ponies of the blend of cordials. Again, my wide pan was alive with blue and orange flames.' When the fire died down, he served the royal party.

The Prince of Wales ate the pancakes with a fork, and then with a spoon scooped up with relish every drop of the remaining syrup. Clearly most impressed, he asked the name of the sweet. 'I told him it was to be called *Crêpes Princesse*. He recognized that the gender was inevitable and that this was a compliment designed for himself, but he protested with mock ferocity that there was a lady present.'

The little girl rose to her feet and curtsied. 'Will you', said the Prince to Charpentier, 'change *Crêpes Princesse* to *Crêpes Suzette?*' And that, according to this great chef, was how a confection was born and baptized that would 'reform a cannibal into a civilized gentleman'. Next day he received a royal reward in the form of a jewelled ring, a Panama hat, and a cane. But what we do not learn, and what still remains a mystery, is little Suzette's surname.

The monarch who loved music most was probably Wagner's patron, Ludwig II of Bavaria. He lived in terror of having to go to the dentist, and so all the food he ate had to be cooked by his chef Theodor Hierneis until it was as soft as possible, and for that reason mince, purées, and omelettes often appeared on the menu. Other dishes were of a more eye-catching kind, many representing Wagnerian characters and scenes. To this end, Hierneis and his assistants spent hours arranging crayfish and lobsters in arresting attitudes on white plaster bases, while Rhine maidens and Valhalla deities fashioned out of tragacanth rose up out of mousses and wild boar pasties.

★
Food on the operatic stage
★

Gourmet meals are served to the characters in many operas. We may assume that the dishes at the Macbeths' banquet would have delighted their guests, and that the Emperor ordered the very best for the picnic in Hans Werner Henze's *We Come to the River*. In the same composer's *Der junge Lord*, Begonia, the Jamaican cook, provides for Sir Edgar's reception the *Croquignoles du diable* that so appealed to Napoleon. The Countess in Richard Strauss's *Capriccio* rewards the two Italians for their singing with a cake, which the soprano finds immensely to her liking.

More fine food is enjoyed by the characters in William Walton's *Troilus and Cressida*, Benjamin Britten's *Death in Venice*, Nino Rota's *Il cappello di paglia di Firenze*, and Gottfried von Einem's *The Visit of the Old Lady* (among the less frequently performed operas) as well as in *The Magic Flute, Fra Diavolo, The Marriage of Figaro, L'elisir d'amore, Salome*, and *Falstaff* (to mention some more familiar works). The Japanese fare for Butterfly's wedding is not appreciated by her American bridegroom, Pinkerton, who describes it as 'flies in aspic and beetles and bumble-bee jelly'. But the food displayed in opera is of course 99 per cent fake and what is real, when tasted, is a grievous disappointment to any gourmet.

It is essential, of course, that comestibles on the stage should resemble the real thing from the front row of the stalls. A lavish banquet is served to Don Giovanni, its scale depending on whether he is shown feasting alone or entertaining a number of bewitching beauties. The backstage experts might supply for this a huge salmon, a superb pheasant, joints of meat, a whole ham, and all kinds of fruit, and the methods adopted for making these vary. The salmon will probably be foam plastic covered with silver lurex, with nylon net used for the fins and tail, pearl sequins for the eyes and two black beads for the pupils. The pheasant might be carved from polystyrene, scrimmed, painted and glazed, or decorated with real feathers; the joints will be made of foam plastic and stretched polystyrene, or of wire frames wrapped in *papier-mâché*, painted and glazed. Gravy can be simulated with blobs of glue, and glue is also coated on the finished 'ham' which is then sprinkled with sawdust to give it the right texture.

The glass which the Don holds during the Champagne Aria is usually empty and just painted yellow; the bubbly served to Prince Orlofsky's guests in *Die Fledermaus* is probably ginger-ale. When, one New Year's Eve, Rudolf Bing treated the cast at the Met to the authentic beverage, they failed to act in the 'morning-after' scene as though suffering from hangovers, and were instead so merry that he decided future New Year celebrations would have to wait until the performance was over.

Edible substances can be set out among the 'property' food if actual eating has to take place – for example, in one production an artificial roast chicken had a lid in its breast with slices of cold chicken concealed inside, which Don Giovanni pretended to tear off the bird and eat with relish. Though the artists would probably enjoy eating caviar in some operatic celebration, all they are likely to be given to represent it is blackcurrant jam. As meat is difficult to swallow when speaking, let alone singing, its place is taken either by bananas sliced length-wise and covered with melted chocolate or cochineal, or bread soaked in gravy, in pink mousse or in jelly. A fried or poached egg is simulated by half an apricot on white blancmange; what looks like an oyster has, disappointingly, nothing in its shell but half a teaspoonful of clear jelly. Practical sandwiches are small, thin, and wet, for dry bread can stick in a singer's throat. In *The Tales of Hoffmann*, those magical many-coloured drinks emanating smoke are produced by dry ice in hot water.

Sometimes food is used for a purpose other than what one might expect. Sir Geraint Evans tells how once when Teresa Berganza appeared in tights as Cherubino at Covent Garden she became exceedingly embarrassed by the conductor's finding her so fetching that he kept winking at her. In the interval she pushed a couple of apples down the front of her breeches, and when she returned to the stage with these additions, he almost dropped his baton.

Cooks themselves appear as characters in some operas. Apart from Begonia in *Der junge Lord*, already mentioned, we have the young pastrycook in Meyerbeer's *Star of the North*, who gives Peter the Great lessons on the flute; and the monastery cook, Brother Boniface, in Massenet's *Le Jongleur de Notre-Dame*. There is a baritone cook in *The Love of Three Oranges*, a tenor one in *Christophe Colomb*, and a mezzo-soprano one in *Le Rossignol*.

Barry Hewlett-Davies in his book *A Night At The Opera* includes the experiences of ballet-dancer Monica Mera when she toured with *La Bohème*. She and others in the *corps* acted as children and urchins playing outside the Café Momus in the second act. Their meagre pay did not permit them to spend much on food, and the real cream cakes, etc., set out on the tables proved so tempting that they would wait in the wings for it to be removed there, then surreptitiously seize all they could and tuck it away down the front of their costumes before dancing on to the stage. As they gambolled around in character, their loot would start seeping through their costumes and their chief concern became to prevent the stage manager from noticing this.

In Wagner's *Parsifal*, Monica and her companions impersonated acolytes whose role in the Grail scene was to enter bearing trays of buns and to go round the long table where the Knights sat, respectfully serving them. While awaiting their cue in the wings, the hungry dancers were tempted into nibbling bits out of the buns. One of the Knights, maintaining with difficulty his devout expression, grumbled in a low voice: 'The rats have had a good go at this – I shall complain to the management.'

If some of the food seen on the stage is not what it seems, neither at times is the food in restaurants. George Rector, the celebrated New York restaurateur, writing from experience during the first two decades of this century, revealed that 'diamond-back terrapin' might be only stewed rabbit in sauce Maryland. Chopped veal often took the place of chicken, and flaked halibut of crab-meat. The sauce would act as camouflage, well laced with sherry. 'Venison stew', out of season, would probably be lamb marinated in claret. 'Next time you order venison,' he suggested, 'ask the waiter to bring you the antlers!'

★

Home is the kitchen

★

In opera's Golden Age, when singers from Europe came to the States to perform in New York, Boston, Philadelphia, Chicago, San Francisco and elsewhere, they missed the dishes to which they had been accustomed at home, or found them so badly cooked that they were travesties of the real thing. They took, therefore, to shopping in the markets, smuggling the raw materials into their bedrooms, and preparing meals on gas rings or portable primus stoves.

One enterprising New York hotel gained the patronage of almost all the foreign artists appearing at the Met by announcing that they permitted cooking in bedrooms and provided facilities for this. As these visitors occupied a whole floor, there were no unappreciative Yankees in the vicinity to object. The stars often even brought their own chefs: Ernestine Schumann-Heink would return to the hotel laden with provisions twice a day, while an Italian tenor's wife, herself a celebrated cook, admitted paying guests to meals served on a card-table in the parlour of the couple's suite.

The American prima donna, Clara Louise Kellogg, claimed that she could often identify the male singer with whom she sang by the odour of his breath alone. Stigelli, she said, reeked of lager, and Mazzolini of the two pounds of cheese he consumed during the day before an evening performance.

Some artists have held the view that the food they eat can affect their acting. For instance, Henry Mossop, a talented but quarrelsome Irish thespian of the eighteenth century who believed this to be true, would eat pork, veal cutlets, or sausages according to whether his role was Richard III, Barbarossa, or Zanga in *The Revenge*. Anfossi, an Italian composer who was his contemporary, held similar opinions and used to work on the scores of his operas in the kitchen, maintaining that he was inspired by the aroma of roasting fowls and sizzling sausages. None of his seventy or so operas have lasted – possibly because of being too light, like the food which helped conceive them.

Bernard Bégué, the French tenor who specialized in playing romantic roles at the Met, also ran a boarding-house on West 39th St, where he did the cooking. He would insist on leaving the rehearsals at mid-day sharp, so that he could rush back to his kitchen and prepare lunch which he also served. His culinary virtuosity became so much admired that many of his fellow singers began to patronize his restaurant, and he eventually went back to France and bought a mansion with the money he had made as a chef.

 # Restaurants with music

★
'The first'

★

La belle époque in Paris could also be described as the 'Banquet Years', which was the title Roger Shattuck gave to his book about the origin of the *avant-garde* in France. The cultural capital of the world, he says, celebrated its vitality over a long table laden with food and wine. 'Bourgeois meals reached such proportions that an intermission had to be introduced in the form of a sherbet course between the two fowl dishes . . . The fashionable salon declined. The café came into its own.'

In the early 1890s a waiter from Reynolds' American Bar borrowed 6,000 francs and started a restaurant not far away, calling it after his given name without its final 'e'. He engaged a capable chef, Chauveau, and an established *maître d'hôtel*, Cornuché, but died some twelve months later, almost down to his last sou. Cornuché took the restaurant over, against his friends' advice. Business remained poor until one evening Irma de Montigny, a popular *femme fatale*, swept in with her entourage and they drank thirty-six bottles of champagne. The new owner was astute enough to see from this how he could turn Maxim's into a money-maker: he must attract to it

Dinner at Maxim's, 1907

glamorous women whose admirers would be lavish spenders.

Cornuché purchased a piano, paid a musician five francs a night to play it, and advertised Maxim's as the first restaurant with music. As he had hoped, professional beauties flocked to Maxim's. To please the men who paid the bills, Cornuché saw to it that they could order almost any dish. The sugar king Lebaudy always wanted a salad of violets, and it was never unavailable. Cornuché had a genius for dealing with difficult clients: one man shouted angrily that there was a beetle in his soup, and Cornuché, hurrying over, put the insect in his mouth and swallowed it, assuring the complainer that it was only a raisin.

No *demi-mondaines* were admitted, except a few borderline cases who were allowed to sit at two tables near the bar. Towards 1 a.m. the carriages would arrive in a steady stream and from them would descend wasp-waisted, bare-shouldered stars of stage and opera, and the *grandes horizontales* – Réjane, Lina Cavalieri, the sisters Jeanne and Anne de Lancy, Jeanne Derval bearing her tiny pet dog in her jewel-encrusted chastity belt, Liane de Pougy, Caroline Otero, and Cléo de Mérode.

Gérard, the chief doorman, looking like a Ruritanian officer in his blue uniform, red cap, and with his eye-glass, would welcome them on entry. He was a man of strong likes and dislikes; those in the latter category, being the largest by far, he called the plagues of his life. He performed many duties: moneylender, confidant, private eye, and go-between.

It was Gérard's resourcefulness that saved Maxim's good name when La Belle Otero, who was a walking jeweller's shop, found that her finest diamond brooch was missing. The doorman's ever-vigilant eye had spotted a stranger brush against her, so he arranged for a waiter to stumble and drop the contents of a dish over the dinner-jacket of the suspect. Then, as Gérard helped to clean the garment, his nimble fingers located and recovered the brooch from a pocket. Obtaining from the chef his most esteemed creation, a soufflé decorated with red roses, Gérard pinned the brooch to the centre rose and set the dessert before the astonished Caroline.

To a corner table at Maxim's the future King Edward VII would bring Lily Langtry when it would have been unwise to be seen with the Jersey Lily publicly in England; while in another corner sometimes sat King Manuel of Portugal with the entrancing Gaby Deslys, and sometimes the Grand Duke Serge with his inamorata, to whom he once presented a pearl necklace costing 2 million francs, tastefully served in a platter of oysters. Upstairs in a private room, Leopold II of Belgium would relax with Cléo de Mérode. More brashly seated in full view of all was the American cotton millionaire who once for dessert asked for, and was brought, a naked girl resting in an ambrosial pink sauce on a silver plateau. Most popular with the other guests was the plate-juggling, flute-playing Baron de Palaud, whose eccentric pranks ranged from entering attended by a string of sandwich men bearing boards advertising cures for kidney complaints, to entertaining a band of circus Red Indians in full war-paint, the sight of whose scalping knives caused panic among some diners.

Caruso and Chaliapin visited Maxim's several times together. The former invariably ate caviar followed by a chicken dish and vegetables, while Chaliapin's choice would be bortsch, a large steak, *pommes soufflées*, and a salad with lemon. Then they shared a soufflé.

An impoverished musician was once unable to pay for the expensive meal he had recklessly eaten. Hugo, the *maître d'hôtel* at the time, knowing the man had a talent for songwriting told him not to worry, and jestingly suggested that he might settle the debt when one of his songs proved a hit. This happened; its title was 'The Girl From Maxim's', and the composer's name was Franz Lehár. Joseph Wechsberg, visiting Maxim's in the early 1950s, interviewed an old waiter who had been there nearly half a century, and asked him whether it was true that, as the words of that song go, customers 'danced upon the tables in and out the spoons'. Léon replied that this was not unusual, and recalled seeing the Vernon Castles dancing the cakewalk on the table top.

In Maxim's safe deposit vault was still kept Hugo's *aide-mémoire*, which Wechsberg was shown. As he relates in his book, *Blue Trout and Black Truffles*, it listed alphabetically 'with almost clinical detachment' the names and addresses of all the fair charmers who frequented the restaurant, together with notes assessing their characters and detailing their tastes and sexual habits. Clearly Hugo intended the contents to be read by posterity, for on the first page is written: 'You, who in the future may peruse the following, ought to know that I refused many offers for the information this book contains, and this refusal saved my honour as *maître d'hôtel*.'

A Mlle L. B. 'lives with her mother, but Mme is hard of hearing'. Mme J. A. 'a beautiful blonde insists that when she says no, she means no. Nevertheless, I still believe that she will change her mind'. Mme A. C. is 'very spoiled by her mother and definitely A.F. except on Tuesdays and Fridays'. Mme R. de L. 'came here for the first time, found her man, and married him. Never came back, what ingratitude.'

Fortunately, Hugo provided a key to the abbreviations he used. This reveals that 'A.F.' meant '*à faire*', while 'R.A.F.', being short for '*rien à faire*', signified that there was nothing doing – though sometimes the qualification '*pour le moment*' is added. 'Y.M.C.A.' was what men pursuing a charmer liked to be told by Hugo, since it stood for '*il y a moyen de coucher avec*', although some of the ladies so described were segregated in a subsection as being allergic to men with moustaches. On a page to themselves were the high-flyers who were only 'A.F.' to those at least of the rank of a grand duke.

Perhaps the most colourful character was a retired cocotte who kept a bar and drove to it every evening in a yellow satin-lined hansom cab. 'Everything is yellow – the hall of her apartment is painted yellow – both her salon and her bedroom are upholstered in yellow, but I heard her bathroom is blood red.'

Roger Shattuck makes a pertinent comment on the morals of this *belle époque*. In his view, the only barrier to rampant adultery was the whalebone corset. 'Many an errant wife, when she returned to face the waiting coachman,' he points out, 'had to hide under her coat the bundle of undergarments which her lover had not been dexterous enough to lace back around her torso.'

Cornuché ran Maxim's with the *savoir faire* of a Quai d'Orsay diplomat and kept a tight rein on any courtesans who might, when over-excited, upset distinguished clients. An exception to this rule was Caroline Otero, whose breasts it was said preceded her 'by a quarter of an hour' and which reminded Colette of 'elongated lemons, firm and upturned at the tips'. (When the Hotel Carlton in Cannes was built, one of Otero's admirers, an architect, used them as models for its twin cupolas, which ever since have been called locally *les boîtes de la Belle Otero*.) At Maxim's, Caroline would leap on to a table and fandango so

'La belle Otero' who boasted that she owned the choicest jewels in France

enticingly that the cartoonist Sem confessed that the sight made
him feel that his thighs were blushing. Her chief rivals were
Lina Cavalieri, then a singing star at the Folies Bergère, and
Liane de Pougy, who once said that the difference between
Caroline Otero and Lina Cavalieri was that when one wore real

jewels they looked false, and that when the other wore false jewels they looked real.

Liane owed her success to Edward VII, when he was Prince of Wales. Before her début at the Folies Bergère, she dared to write and ask him to be present and to applaud her. Amused by the nerve of this complete stranger, he complied. Soon men were fighting for her favours and she could afford to buy emerald rings for her toes, wearing them when in bed. Both she and Caroline Otero boasted that they owned the choicest jewels in France, and it was agreed that they should bring their collections one night to Maxim's and allow its habitués to judge. La Belle Otero was the first to arrive, loaded with her loot from dazzling diadem on ebony locks to the gem-decorated heels of her twinkling slippers. Her victory seemed certain, for only her arrogant face was left uncovered by this costly and challenging carapace.

But soon afterwards the door opened and the slim, aristocratic figure of Liane de Pougy appeared, dressed entirely in black which showed to best advantage her white skin and exquisitely delicate features. Not a single jewel did she display. Behind her came her personal maid, who removed the coat she was wearing and, in the words of an onlooker, resembled an illuminated Eiffel Tower. As abounding applause proclaimed de Pougy's triumph, a raging Otero rushed menacingly towards the winner and had to be restrained.

Tiring of appearing at the Folies Bergère, Caroline Otero decided in 1912 to start a new career in grand opera, and after twenty-six singing lessons she made her début in June that year at the *Trente Ans du Théâtre aux Variétés* playing the title role in the first act of *Carmen*. It was type-casting, and most of the critics praised her. Professional opera-singers, however, were furious that a music-hall dancer should dare to poach on their preserve, and that not only should she gain the critics' approval but also attract packed audiences. Their jealousy erupted into open hostility when it became known that Otero's backers were taking over the Opéra de Nice so that she might star in *Cavalleria Rusticana*, *La Navarraise*, and *Tosca*, in addition to

Carmen. Their trade union went to law and she was ordered by the court not to sing in such roles, as there were already a sufficient number of professionals capable of doing this in her stead, and who were unemployed.

In his reminiscences, *Steeplejack*, James Gibbons Huneker gave a vivid description of his first visit to Maxim's. He wrote:

A red-haired woman who looked like a big salacious Chéret poster furiously waltzed and sprawled and slid as the gypsy band vertiginously played. She had in tow a little chap whose eyes bulged with joy and realized ambition. He possessed the largest lady in the building; what more could he expect! The band was wonderful. It ripped and buzzed with rhythmic rubato rage, and tore Czardas passion to ragtime tatters. It leered, sang, swooned, sighed, snarled, sobbed, and leaped. Its leader, a dark gypsy with a wide, bold glance, swayed as he smote the strings with his bow . . . The moral weather was scarlet, the toilettes admirable. Occasionally there strayed in British tourists, but if they had their womenfolk with them they fled; if not, they remained. I saw nothing objectionable; the establishment simply overflowed with good-humoured devilry. The tone was unmistakably scarlet, and as the night wore apace it became a rich carmilion – a color said to be a compound of carmine and vermilion; also of lobster, champagne, and rouge.

Paul Valéry's description of Maxim's was briefer, but brilliant. He said it reminded him of a submarine that had been sunk with all its period trappings.

In 1913 Maxim's celebrated its twentieth birthday with a dinner for which the fare was: *Melon Glacé – Lobster – Smoked Salmon – Tartlets with Parmesan – Chicken Consommé – Carpe Braisé à la Chambord – Porc Farci à l'Alsacienne – Ragoût of Truffles – Poularde Maxim's – Salad – Asparagus with Sauce Hollandaise – Dessert*. It seems a pity that no dish was named after any of the fascinating characters who gave the place its allure. The First World War drained it of all glamour, and later, bought by a London firm in 1932, it became so respectable that no husband needed to have any qualms about bringing his wife there, no matter how straitlaced she might be. When, with the fall of France, the Germans occupied Paris, leading Nazis like Goering and Goebbels haunted it. As a result, the 50th anniversary was not observed until 1949; the gala dinner menu then included *Lobster Belle Otero*, *Chicken Merry Widow* and *Glace Belle Époque*.

Today, Maxim's is owned by Pierre Cardin. On a truly enchanted evening there, he held a party in honour of Dame Kiri Te Kanawa who sang to his guests.

★

Built by music

★

With the profits he made by presenting early Gilbert and Sullivan operas, Richard D'Oyly Carte bought some waste land between the Strand and the Thames Embankment and built the first theatre with electric lighting, the Savoy Theatre. It opened in October 1881 with *Patience*, which transferred there from the Opéra Comique in the East Strand and continued to draw the town. It was followed by *Iolanthe*, and other box-office successes. Visiting the United States to try and prevent pirating, D'Oyly Carte was impressed by the comfort of American hotels, finding them superior to anything in London. This gave him the idea of erecting one, together with a restaurant open to the public, next door to his theatre. The land was available and five years later, in 1889, the building was completed.

Carte decided that it was vitally important for the new hotel to have a manager and a chef of sufficient calibre not only to attract visitors initially but to ensure that they returned there whenever they were in London. On the Continent César Ritz, a former Swiss waiter with ambitions to excel as an hotelier, had since 1883 been successfully running the Grand Hotel, Monte Carlo and the Grand National, Lucerne. As *chef de cuisine* he had a young Frenchman, Georges Auguste Escoffier, destined to be regarded as the greatest of gastronomic experts. They were helped enormously from the start of their joint association by the Prince of Wales for whom Escoffier had created a masterpiece of a dish, *Poularde Derby*, when the future King Edward VII was staying at the Grand National. So impressed was the Prince of Wales with both the hotel's service and its cuisine that from then onwards he patronized all their hotels and restaurants, and the British aristocracy followed his example.

In 1887 Ritz took over the Restaurant de la Conversation in Baden-Baden, where he mounted a sumptuous dinner party for a German prince. D'Oyly Carte, who was taking the cure, attended it. Nothing could be faulted and he was so pleased that he instantly offered the post of manager at the Savoy to Ritz, who turned down the offer. Six months after the Savoy opened, things were in such bad shape that Carte, in desperation, again approached him and proposed such temptingly attractive terms that he yielded. Once Ritz had brought order into what had been near chaos, he sent for Escoffier who proceeded to carry out revolutionary changes in the kitchens.

'If you happen to be a potato,' Escoffier told the cooks he trained, 'don't pretend to be a turnip. Be yourself. And whatever you have to cook must be the same: let it be its best, of course, but always itself. Never attempt to hide or camouflage food; your job is to see that it is dressed properly, not overdressed, and certainly not masquerading as something that it never was expected to be.'

The reputation that Ritz and Escoffier had already won for themselves abroad assured for the Savoy the patronage of foreign epicures coming to London, and business swiftly improved. But neither man could relax for a moment. To keep gourmets as regular visitors required not only the highest standards of cuisine but the constant creation of new dishes. Escoffier had to make certain that whenever clients arrived –

Georges Auguste Escoffier, one of the greatest and most creative of chefs

and no matter how unexpectedly – the food they liked most could readily be supplied. He also had to bear in mind that for those with business appointments to keep or who were on their way to the opera or the theatre, swift service was essential. This called for complete dedication to his *métier* and for genius at planning, and throughout his eighteen-hour day Escoffier displayed both. He consequently saw little of his wife, and within a few months, further depressed by the English climate, she went to live in Monaco; he remained on his own until his retirement in 1919.

Staff had to be carefully trained, and they sometimes failed. Escoffier regarded as the worst disaster of his life the evening when a clumsy waiter serving peas dropped them down a lady's corsage. Panic-stricken, the culprit began with fumbling fingers to pick the peas off her, and was then felled by the furious husband.

But it was having constantly to create new dishes that Escoffier found his most difficult challenge. He was to write in his *Guide Culinaire*:

Novelty! It is the prevailing cry; it is imperiously demanded by everyone. For all that, the number of alimentary substances is comparatively small, the number of their combinations is not infinite, and the amount of raw material placed either by art or nature at the disposal of a cook does not grow in proportion to the whims of the public. What feats of ingenuity have we not been forced to perform at times in order to meet our customer's wishes! Only those who have had charge of a large kitchen can tell the tale. Personally, I have ceased counting the nights spent in the attempt to discover new combinations, when completely broken with the fatigue of a heavy day, my body ought to have been at rest. Yet the chef who has had the felicity to succeed in turning out an original and skilful preparation approved by his public and producing a vogue cannot, even for a time, claim the monopoly of his secret discovery or derive any benefit therefrom.

Earlier great chefs such as Carême and Alexis Soyer had made quantity and a magnificent appearance the main features of their cuisine. Escoffier, by contrast, believed in quality first, and in fewer dishes, as an ever speedier style of life required.

Until he began reforming gastronomy, his own famous quip was true: 'If you want to keep your appetite, keep out of the kitchen.' Authors of earlier cookery books had taken this for granted: Mme Ayläe Adamson told her readers that they 'must not throw the scum behind the stove, but put it aside for the dog's soup'. Escoffier's concern was that a diner should be able to digest easily all the food that was served, and only combinations of ingredients that passed this essential test were used in his recipes. He rejected all that was implied by the adage: '*La sauce fait passer le poisson.*' The fish content of his dishes was never of inferior quality to the sauce, though it was not that he neglected the latter. He had a rare facility for devising delicious new flavours, believing that the kitchen is a country in which there are always discoveries to be made.

Escoffier, a blacksmith's son, was dubbed the 'Emperor of Cooks' by Kaiser Wilhelm II; and another Emperor, Napoleon III, exiled in England, agreed at least about that with the son of the Prussian who had defeated him. Escoffier was no linguist, and enjoyed jesting that he refused to take any English lessons for fear that his cooking might also become Anglicized. A little man, he wore high heels so as to get a better view of all that was cooking on the ranges, and he rarely tasted anything but sniffed instead, believing that was the truest guide.

Escoffier and César Ritz were the first in the catering world whose priority was to please their women guests. Escoffier especially admired great actresses and divas, like Sarah Bernhardt, Adelina Patti, and Nellie Melba. They became his friends and many of his dishes were named after them.

César Ritz noticed one striking difference between restaurants on the other side of the Channel and that of the Savoy. The English ate in relative silence and, he was sure, drank less wine and left sooner as a result. A background of music, he decided, might make the customers spend more time and more money in the restaurant. He experimented by engaging Johann Strauss and his orchestra, and soon the increased takings from the sales of wine alone paid for the cost of the musicians.

The Savoy owed its existence to Arthur Sullivan's music and, thanks to its proximity to Covent Garden, it soon became the London home of opera stars – such as Caruso who, after a huge supper, might entertain the waiters by his popular trick of shifting a piano by inflating his chest against it.

The most spectacular dinner party to be held at the Savoy took place on 30 June 1905 when George A. Kessler, the champagne millionaire at the head of Moët et Chandon in Europe and America, celebrated King Edward VII's birthday. The forecourt to the east entrance was enclosed and filled with water four feet deep and dyed blue, and was encircled by scenery depicting St Mark's, the Doge's Palace and its sur-roundings, lit by some 400 Venetian lamps. Into the water had been released salmon trout and whitebait, whilst on it floated swans, ducks, and a white, silk-lined gondola adorned with 31,000 carnations, roses and 5,000 yards of smilax. In the air above fluttered a hundred white doves.

Waiters costumed as gondoliers served twelve courses to twice that number of diners seated on gold chairs, who included Mme Réjane from Paris and the 'Belle of New York', Edna May. The *maître chef*, Thoraud, surpassed himself in the visual appeal and gastronomic excellence of the fare provided. Three impressive lions carved out of ice bore trays of peaches and glacé fruits; and at the finish a baby elephant carried a foot-tall, candle-lit birthday cake over a bridge from *terra firma* to the gondola. It was followed by a bevy of Gaiety girls drinking the health of the monarch in Moët et Chandon champagne.

Throughout the banquet an orchestra stationed in a smaller gondola played music. Then came a *coup de théâtre*. The lights dimmed as a melon-like moon, suspended overhead, was turned on and Caruso emerged through brocade curtains at the raised end of the gondola to sing – for a *douceur* of £450.

Many composers also stayed and ate at the Savoy, among them Leoncavallo and Puccini when preparing for the London premières of *I Zingari* and *Manon Lescaut* respectively. Pietro Mascagni arrived with a trunk containing dozens of dress shirts and nearly 200 collars: he always travelled well-stocked with these, for podium perspiration caused many changes during the evening, and he would trust no laundry but one in Leghorn to send back his laundry stiff to the eye yet pliant enough not to hinder his movements. In January 1922 Richard Strauss took a suite at the Savoy and soon complained that it was overheated. A window was opened, admitting thick, yellow fog. 'I have represented fog musically,' he said with a smile to the puzzled chambermaid.

Daly's theatre was also close at hand, and after *The Merry Widow*'s triumphant first night there Franz Lehár confessed to Lily Elsie and George Graves, over Tokay at a celebratory Savoy supper, that he had never achieved his real ambition, which was to become a great violinist. He had given up the struggle when Dvorak wearying of his friend's scraping had told him frankly that he was wasting his time, advising instead: 'Nail your fiddle to the wall and try to become a composer!'

Another musical-comedy star, José Collins, had a suite at the Savoy. She was of such an impulsive nature that when some women friends admired her ranch mink cloak, she borrowed a carving knife, cut it up, gave each a portion and what was left to the chambermaid.

In 1910 the Ballets Russes first came to Covent Garden and Diaghilev joined the artistic luminaries filling the Savoy. Though it was midsummer, he rarely appeared without his fur-collared overcoat and a homburg shading his heavily lidded eyes. Light flashed from the array of rings on his fingers and from his large tiepin, as he ate his way through a multitude of courses and expatiated on his fancied ailments. Also easily recognizable was 'Tommy' Beecham, clearly the idol of his regular companion, Lady Cunard. But a conductor uninterested in the glories of the menu was Toscanini, whose meagre repast would be limited to fruit and a glass of wine before he slipped away early to bed.

Ritz and Escoffier actually remained only seven years at the Savoy, then for various reasons they left and opened the Ritz Hotel in Paris. Aristocratic elegance and the best in modern comfort soon made it the premier hotel in the world. In the kitchens, however, Escoffier still used charcoal and coal, maintaining that grilling and roasting with those fuels gave a far better flavour than with gas and electricity. For pots and pans, too, he preferred old-fashioned copper and was contemptuous of aluminium.

★
The Carlton
★

Having established the hotel named after him in Paris, César Ritz opened the Carlton Hotel next door to Her Majesty's Theatre in the Haymarket on 1 July 1899. Six months earlier, Escoffier had begun to organize the new hotel's cuisine, with the object of providing *à la carte* food for the first time in England, and on an unprecedentedly large scale. No fewer than sixty cooks were engaged, and within a short while the Carlton was regarded by London society as the most exhilarating eating-place in the capital. Tables had to be reserved well ahead as it was invariably full for luncheon and dinner, up to 500 diners being served on Sundays. Even at tea-time there was animation not to be found elsewhere. Undoubtedly the carefully chosen orchestra and its music contributed in no small measure to the Carlton's success, as it continued to do at the Savoy where Renato Piovanelli was then restaurant manager and engaged Franz Vecsey, the Austrian violinist and winner of the first prize at the Viennese Conservatoire. Vecsey's art and his attractive personality endeared him to the Savoy's clientèle, who showed their appreciation with gifts of gold sovereigns which he would altruistically fling on to the piano to be shared among the other musicians.

As R. J. Minney wrote in *The Edwardian Age*, for sixpence less than three pounds two people could feast at the Carlton on a seven-course dinner, beginning with oyster soup and followed by fillet of sole (served in piecrust with vermicelli and crayfish tails, flavoured with champagne and parmesan); *noisettes de*

César Ritz, hotelier, whose name became a household
word to describe the grandly opulent

chevreuil Diane; suprême de volaille au paprika; ortolans cooked in an earthenware cocotte and served with grapes as a foundation; *friandises* and Benedictine-flavoured cherries in a pink casing. The price included champagne and coffee. All would be served to the couple as they reclined in large armchairs in the cream and pink lounge, 'where a pale blue light fell on the palms and a band played a Hungarian march or a mazurka'.

Escoffier was never at a loss dealing with difficult diners. A German aristocrat once asked for *bécasse flambée à l'eau de Cologne* and the Emperor of Cooks produced it. His recipe was the same as for woodcock Fine Champagne, but instead of a liqueur brandy he used Eau de Cologne 4711.

★
Delmonico's

★

When G. M. Pullman launched his first sumptuous dining-car on the American railroads, he named it the 'Delmonico'. It was a tribute to the family which was responsible more than any other for introducing gourmet cooking to the western hemisphere. In 1825 Ticino-born John Delmonico, skipper of a schooner based on New York, tired of seafaring and opened a store on the Battery where he sold fine imported wines. Here he was joined by his brother Peter, who had managed a *pâtisserie* in Berne, and two years later they opened a café on William St where pastries, ice-cream and liquid refreshments could be eaten on the premises. This proved so profitable that they engaged a French chef and fitted out the place as a proper restaurant; such choice dishes were served that soon, owing to lack of space, would-be customers were constantly being turned away.

In 1832, the brothers were joined by their nineteen-year-old nephew from Switzerland, Lorenzo, who was to prove a brilliant restaurateur. He was put in charge of a second establishment, built on Broad St, where the success-story continued and where his own three younger brothers, Siro, François, and Constant, came to help him run it. When a fire destroyed the William St premises, a larger plot was bought at 2 South William St, and here there arose a building on three floors, with a café and a restaurant at ground-level and with a ballroom and lounges which the press lauded as the most splendid and comfortable of their kind in the United States. Much was made of the impressive entrance adorned on either side by two marble pillars from Pompeii.

In 1845, the second Delmonico's also burned down, and the following year it was replaced by a five-storey restaurant at 21–23 Broadway under Siro's supervision, which became a special favourite with musicians. Here Jenny Lind would sup after singing at concerts in 1850 and 1851. But the place was too far downtown to be fashionable, so in 1853 Lorenzo sold it and moved up Broadway to the corner of Chambon Street. He had already engaged a brilliant young chef, Charles Ranhofer, who was to reign over the firm's kitchens for thirty-four years and who later consolidated his reputation by publishing his collection of over 4,000 recipes, *The Epicurean*.

The Delmonico restaurants were the focal points of New York's gastronomic life in the nineteenth century. Lorenzo took personal charge of the purchase of provisions, rising at dawn to visit the Washington and Fulton Fish Markets. In 1876, when getting on in years, he opened another gourmet restaurant in Madison Square, which flourished under the management of his nephew Charles, and which the *Tribune* called 'the pride of the nation'. Twenty-one years later, when that neighbourhood had become too garish for elegant patrons, a larger and grander rendezvous for them was erected on the corner of Fifth Avenue and 44th St. Respectability ruled. No man was permitted to eat alone with a woman in the private rooms, all of which had to have their doors left open and which were regularly visited by the staff to ensure that nothing improper was taking place.

Even so influential and valuable a client as August Belmont

Supper after the play at Delmonico's, 1898, by Albert
Sterner

was not exempt from such restrictions. He and his wife had
arranged to entertain a couple in a private room, but because of
a confusion over the date the guests failed to arrive – so the
head-waiter refused to serve the Belmonts. The banker demanded to see Charles Delmonico who courteously but firmly
refused to make an exception for them. Rather than walk out of
their favourite restaurant, the couple reluctantly ate in the
public dining-room.

It was a king of snobs, Ward McAllister, who masterminded
in Delmonico's ballroom a number of 'cotillion dinners' limited
to a hundred subscribers of whom he approved. Until then such
society functions had always been held in private mansions, but
this experiment proved so successful that hostesses began
hiring suitable ballrooms for their revels.

Playful Mrs Pierre Lorillard Ronalds was one öf the first to hold a spectacular costume ball at Delmonico's, at which supper was served until 5 a.m. and the orchestra played for a further hour. She dressed to represent 'Music': her gown was embroidered with the score of an Italian ballet, and on her head she flaunted a tiara composed of musical notes grouped around a harp, from jets in which flickered flames that were fed by a gas cylinder concealed by false hair. The reporters next day, describing the sensation all this caused, also drew attention to her short dress and scarlet boots encircled by tiny, tinkling bells, which were identical with those worn by some women of easy virtue in Water St. This upset the Delmonicos greatly.

In view of the care that was taken to maintain the tone of this citadel of elegant eating it is perhaps surprising that no objection should have been taken to the activities of a regular customer, Colonel D'Alton Mann – unless, perhaps, he knew of some skeleton in Delmonico's cupboard. It was true that the Colonel's long white beard, clerical frock coat, dignified appearance, and perfect manners made one feel sure he was a gentleman one could trust with anything. But quite the reverse was true, for he was the proprietor and editor of a notorious weekly magazine, *Town Topics*, that filled its columns with scandal supplied by an army of paid spies ranging from telegraphists to domestics employed by those in high society.

Desperate were the measures the Colonel's prey sometimes adopted to preserve their privacy, the most ingenious being that of oil millionairess Mrs Ann Archibald, who installed in her Bar Harbor summer home a dining-room table the centre section of which, operated by a motor, travelled down through the floor to the kitchen below, removing what was no longer needed and bringing up each new course in turn. This meant that hostess and guests could talk freely without danger from eavesdropping servants.

Although *Town Topics* gained a wide circulation, those revelations that would have been the most sensational were rarely published. When the copy had been set up in print, the Colonel would make for Delmonico's with the galley proofs and seat himself at a reserved table near the entrance, where he could spot his quarry's arrival at once. While waiting, he usually ate six double Southdown mutton chops served with liver, kidneys and baked yams, and well irrigated by a bottle of the best champagne. To the amusement of those in his vicinity, he made often appreciative 'Woof-woof!' noises.

When the person whom the Colonel was seeking came in, accompanied by wife or other guest, the Colonel would give him time to get settled, then tip a page to go up to him and say he was wanted urgently on the telephone in the bar. There the Colonel would be already installed with two glasses and another bottle of champagne. 'Just the fellow I want to see!' he would exclaim with a pleasant smile. 'I was leaving for lunch when this proof turned up from the composing-room. It's about you, so I'd like you to cast your eye over it.'

Dismayed by what he read, the other would readily agree to 'lend' the Colonel $500, in return for which he would be given the galley proof and assured that the story would never be published or more money demanded. D'Alton Mann always kept his word, and some people even regarded it as a sort of compliment to be considered of sufficient importance to merit his attention.

When banquets took place in Delmonico's spacious ballroom it could, if the occasion demanded, be almost filled by a huge table reputed to be the largest in New York. It was here that millionaire importer Edward Cuckemeyer, affronted at being cold-shouldered by high society, held a dinner party for seventy-two guests that become known as the 'Swan Banquet'. Having unexpectedly been refunded some $10,000 in customs duty through an incorrect assessment, Cuckemeyer jested that the banquet had been paid for by the government. The news-papers carried detailed accounts of the event: 'Every inch of the oval table was covered with flowers, excepting a place in the centre, left for a lake, and a border around the table for the plates.' The lake was thirty feet long and nearly as wide as the table, and was covered by a golden wire cage reaching to the ceiling. 'Four superb swans brought from Prospect Park swam here, surrounded by high banks of flowers of every species and variety, which prevented them from splashing the water on the table. There were hills and dales, the modest little violet carpeting the valleys, and other bolder sorts climbing up and covering the tops of these miniature mountains.' From the ceiling hung a glittering array of golden cages full of songbirds. Their music, Cuckemeyer told a guest, he found far more attractively natural than all the warblings at the Met. The only contretemps caused briefly was 'a fierce combat' between the swans.

Several celebrated 'canaries' also ate at Delmonico's, among them Emma Eames, who at one time was Melba's rival, and who was the toast of New York operatic circles for her Juliet in Gounod's *Roméo et Juliette*. She wrote in *Some Memories and Reflexions* that in the early 'nineties it was 'one of the most delightful places' to meet friends. There were two dining-rooms on the main floor, 'the one on the right being the haven of business men who wanted to eat, smoke and talk undisturbed, and the other on the left, the meeting-place of those who were ready to take life less seriously'. These were never noisy or overcrowded, and in them one was served 'delicious food, as delicious as any in France, by servants perfectly trained'. But, unfortunately, according to her, 'the curious and the trippers and the climbers soon transformed this delightful place into a bedlam'.

★

Sherry's

★

In 1890 Louis Sherry, proprietor of a confectioner's shop not far from the Metropolitan Opera House in New York, succeeded in gaining the concession to provide catering for the audience during the intervals. His efficiency and the quality of the fare he provided so pleased opera-goers that the wealthy among them employed him to do the same for their own private parties. Delmonico's was faced with a determined rival the day Sherry left his Sixth Avenue location and opened a luxurious restaurant of similar style to theirs on Fifth Avenue and 37th St. His first major success came when the organizers of the prestigious Patriarchs' Balls deserted the older establishment and decided to hold them on his premises in future.

The competition with Delmonico's continued relentlessly. One year Sherry's would prove the most popular with high society, the next year it would be the reverse. In October 1898, Sherry's moved into a twelve-storey building on the south-west corner of Fifth Avenue and 44th St, diagonally opposite its rival, and there two years later Cornelius K. G. Billing celebrated the completion of his $200,000 stable by holding a 'Horseback Dinner'. Thirty livery-stable nags were coaxed one by one into the freight elevator and taken up to the grand ballroom on the fourth floor, where the host and his guests mounted them and dined off tables fastened to the animals' withers, and drank champagne through rubber tubes connected to saddle-bags hanging on the horses' flanks. Meanwhile, the waiters dressed as grooms fed oats to the horses when they were not occupied in serving a fourteen-course dinner to the guests.

In 1896 Sherry's was the scene of 'The Awful Seeley Dinner' which scandalized New York and for a time tarnished the restaurant's reputation. The 'hootchy-kootchy' dancer Little Egypt was served practically naked in a pie, and the dinner was raided by the police. Another contretemps occurred in 1905, when Laura Swann's fabulous hat caught fire.

The most spectacular dinner ever held there took place on 31 January 1914, when the millionaire Francophile James Hazen Hyde commissioned Whitney Warren to transform Sherry's for the night into a make-believe Palace of Versailles. Three hundred and fifty guests danced to eighteenth-century music played by the Met's 40-piece orchestra and were entertained by its entire *corps de ballet*. At midnight the famous actress Mme Réjane arrived in a sedan chair, followed by her artists, and performed a French bedroom farce against scenery shipped from Paris. After polite applause by the guests, few of whom had understood a word, Hyde led them down to supper on the second floor, which had been converted into a replica of a garden in the style of Versailles with a real lawn under foot, roses, trailing everywhere, flowering shrubs, suspended cherubs, marble statues, and iluminated fountains. Before the *Consommé Voltaire* was served, Mme Réjane rose from her chair on Hyde's right and recited a poem about Franco–American friendship which was toasted with Pol Roger 1889. After the meal there was more dancing upstairs, followed by a second supper at 3 a.m. Only one guest did not dance and that was Mrs Clarence Mackay who had come dressed as Adrienne Lecouvreur playing Phèdre and who, despite the assistance of two negro boys in pink brocade, could hardly move owing to the weight of her long silver-cloth train. Eventually, in desperation, she cut it off and sent the boys home with it and her sceptre.

The last to linger towards 7 a.m. was Mrs Joseph Widener who told Hyde: 'You have given us a most delightful eighteenth-century dinner, but I think the time is ripe for a little twentieth-century breakfast.'

'What would you like?' he asked.

'Fishballs!' she replied, hopefully.

★
The first lobster palace
★

When William Waldorf Astor turned his back on his homeland to settle in England, he made up his mind to humiliate those who had prevented him from achieving his ambition – the voters who, contrary to his expectations, had not elected him to Congress, and his arrogant aunt, Mrs Astor, whom he had failed to dislodge as leader of New York society. Her splendid residence, dominating the south-west corner of Fifth Avenue and 34th St, stood in extensive grounds separating it from the mansion which he had inherited. In 1893, to punish that snobbish aunt and reduce the value of other properties in the neighbourhood owned by those who had rejected him, William Astor had his father's house razed to the ground and replaced by a hotel, thirteen storeys high, that made all the pompous brownstones look like insignificant pigmies.

Astor then leased the hotel to George C. Boldt, an enterprising hotelier who had already gained for the Bellevue, his small hotel on Philadelphia's Broad Street, the reputation of having the finest cuisine in America. Boldt's policy was to make the Waldorf sumptuous enough to equal any Fifth Avenue mansion. To attract the right clientèle, he persuaded prominent socialites to organize in aid of a fashionable charity the concert held in the hotel at its formal opening on 13 March 1893. Mrs William Kissan Vanderbilt engaged the New York Symphony Orchestra, which played in the luxurious main restaurant, later called the Empire Room. Over 4,000 tickets were sold at the then colossal sum of $5 each, but only 1,500 ticket-holders could be comfortably accommodated, so the doors were locked as soon as that number had entered.

Those excluded found so much of interest in the rest of the hotel that no one complained. The *Herald* reported next day: 'All swelldom inspected the house from top to bottom and then ate a fine supper.' At that time, with hardly any European period furniture in the country, what attracted the most attention were the furniture and tapestries in the 'State Apartments' – reproductions of those once owned by King François I, preserved in the Musée de Cluny, and which cost $35,000. The *Sun* gushed: 'Louis XIV could not have got the likes of the first suite of apartments set apart for the most distinguished guests of the hotel. There is a canopied bed upon a dais, such as a king's should be. Upon this couch shall repose the greatnesses and, looking about them, see many thousands of dollars' worth of fineries. Think of the joy of being great!'

Impressed with what it had examined and eaten, New York society now made a regular habit of dining at the Waldorf, and those whom curiosity had attracted to the opening from Phila-delphia, Boston, and Baltimore decided always to stay there when visiting the city. Boldt was determined to make his restaurants more attractive than any others: he was the first in America to have arrangements of flowers on every table, as well as candelabra. In the exclusive Palm Room white tie and tails for men and evening gowns for ladies were obligatory wear, and reserving a table there became as difficult as getting a box at the Met. A glass wall separated the Palm Room from the Palm Garden, where afternoon tea was served while six Tyroleans in costume danced and yodelled.

As William Waldorf Astor had hoped, his aunt, Mrs Astor, was outraged by his *lèse-majesté* in having such a caravanserai next door to her, and so she ordered the best architect available to build her an ostentatious new home well up town and far removed from anything so vulgar as an hotel. Despite her anger, however, she did not want to suffer financially on account of her forced move, and wily George C. Boldt per-suaded her and her son the most advantageous way to exploit the financial potential of the vacated house was to demolish it too, and use the site for another hotel, which could then be let as an annexe to the Waldorf on profit-sharing terms.

The son scored off his cousin by building the Astoria four storeys higher than the Waldorf, and, although the two hotels were to be run as one, a legal provision was made that allowed him at any time to require every connecting passage to be bricked up – thus enabling him to break the partnership at short notice.

The second hotel opened in November 1897, and was as ostentatious as its neighbour. Every private parlour flaunted a gold grand piano supplied by the manufacturer Charles Stein-way (who was also a gourmet and was later famous for the musical banquet lasting several hours which he held there). The public at large refused to regard the two hotels as separate entities, and Boldt himself was responsible for inserting the hyphen between their names: he thought 'Waldorf-Astoria' sounded imposing and would catch the eye at once in advertisements.

One of the Waldorf-Astoria's great attractions was its magnificent ballroom which could be used either for banquets or for concerts at which some 1,500 persons could sit comfortably. A series of such concerts were held under the baton of the celebrated conductor and Wagnerian, Anton Seidl, in the style of German court musicales. The snob appeal of such performances ensured full audiences, and for the season those with social pretensions gladly paid $60 for a single seat on the floor and $350 for a box, to listen to star singers like Edouard de Reszke, Enrico Caruso, Pol Plançon, Nellie Melba, Emma Calvé, Emma Eames, and Lillian Nordica.

When these feasts of song lost their novelty, they were succeeded by weekly Monday musicales, and Liszt's pupil Albert M. Bagby gave a new look to the recitals by lecturing on music in an entertaining as well as an illuminating manner. As these were held in the morning, most of the audience would stay on for luncheon. On 21 January 1895 Victor Herbert and his own orchestra had played for the first time in the Waldorf, and were so acclaimed that they returned on several other occasions. He was one of the happiest and most engaging of composers, and his wife, Thérèse Herbert-Förster, was known far and wide as a mistress of the culinary art.

The Waldorf-Astoria's principal restaurant was approached from the carriage entrance by a long, wide corridor along which, in all their finery, the socialites would strut. An editor of the *Tribune* dubbed this route of high fashion the 'Peacock Alley', and it became one of the sights of America. For hours, women packed sofas and chairs on either side, gaping enviously at the gowns, the hats, and the furs of the fashionable and the wealthy. At the peak of its popularity, up to 25,000 people a day would pass through the Peacock Alley, which became so famous that foreigners assumed it was a street in New York and addressed mail to it.

Concerts by a brilliant orchestra were given in the main foyer on Sunday evenings, when Alley addicts could confidently expect the city's most celebrated visitors from abroad to be on view, too, for close inspection. Not surprisingly, it was said that staying at the Waldorf-Astoria was like being a goldfish in a glass bowl.

This public palace's *maître d'hôtel* was a tall and burly Swiss, Oscar Tschirky, who had the appearance of an imposing operatic tenor and who was in his element when, after premières at the Met, its 'Diamond Horseshoe' came in strength to sup. Often some 800 portions of Lobster Newburg alone would be served. Oscar once expressed his feelings about his work thus:

> To eat one's fill merely to appease one's appetite without finesse or selection is an avowal of barbarism worthy only of the wild beast or savage. To savour and enjoy a banquet – one of our modern achievements of culinary art and imaginative effect – implies an enviable degree of rare development in mind and manners.
>
> I admit freely that when I am called upon to tempt the appetite of a cultured gastronomic organ where eye and ear must serve as a whet, I receive my greatest delight and inspiration. Add to this order that other *carte blanche* – which lays no limit upon expenditure – then indeed one realizes that he has received a summons to create a work of artistic good cheer that should live in the memory of every participant. I have made it a rule, whatever the purpose of the feast, to work out my dinner with a settled design, what musicians call *leitmotif*.

If asked what precisely he meant by this reference to a recurring theme, Oscar might well have given as an example the dinner he prepared for leading New York politician Randolph Guggenheimer, when he entertained forty members of the Tammany Hall fraternity and their wives to a feast costing more than $10,000. The banqueting room was transformed into the semblance of a highly fanciful garden, with bunches of hot-house grapes decoratively suspended from lattice work, together with ornate cages in which songbirds competed to

out-trill one another. There were American Beauty roses everywhere in full bloom, and an illuminated pool lay in the centre of
the table surrounded by massed orchids, lilies, acacia, and more
roses. On the napkins sparkled jewelled crystal scent-bottles for
the ladies, and for the men gem-studded matchbox-holders.
The *hors d'oeuvres* were so garnished as to create the impression
that it was high summer and this theme was repeated throughout the meal.

Thousands of bottles of a celebrated sauce of Oscar's devising
were prepared in the hotel's kitchens and marketed, stressing
that only he knew the ingredients. Not so secret was the recipe
for Waldorf Salad, that mixture of chopped apples, celery, and
walnuts resting on a bed of lettuce.

French visitors would say that the only bread in America as
good as that to which they were used at home were the rolls
served at the Waldorf-Astoria. Oscar once revealed his method:
'Mix a quart of flour with a little salt and two eggs, a tablespoon-
ful of lard and two of yeast with enough milk to make a good
dough. Work it and set it out to rise for the night. In the
morning, work it thoroughly again and form it into rolls. Let
these rise again, and bake them in a quick oven.'

In the autumn of 1904 the St Regis opened. It was managed
by a Hungarian, R. M. Haan, who brought from Paris Edmond
Baily, destined to be regarded as one of the most accomplished
cooks in the United States. From then onwards, hotel after
hotel sprang up north of 42nd St in the Fifth Avenue district.
The following year, the Gotham was built right opposite it; in
1906 the Belmont rose on 42nd St and the Knickerbocker
climbed into the sky as well. Hardly twelve months later yet
another competitor appeared – the Plaza. This was to become
known as the home of thirty-nine enormously rich widows, one
of whom for the last decade of her life had her Rolls and liveried
chauffeur awaiting her outside every morning, until twelve
o'clock struck. Then madam's personal maid would send down
a message that her mistress had decided not to go out that day.
For the whole of those ten years the widow was, in fact,
completely bedridden.

All these rivals acted like leeches draining away the Waldorf-Astoria's life-blood; and by the time Boldt died in 1916 it looked as if the famous hotel might not outlast him long. Lucius Boomer, with the financial backing of General Coleman Du Pont, tried hard to keep it alive, but it had become too old-fashioned and uneconomic to run and guests were complaining about the vibrations caused by trains rumbling on the tracks below. So the first of the lobster palaces was torn down, and the present hotel was built on the site with elaborate precautions to cushion it against the railroad noises. The new Waldorf-Astoria opened on 1 October 1931, and owing to the economic depression it could not have done so at a worse time. In fact, it was already bankrupt and its bonds were sold in bundles which buyers did not bother to count. Mrs Boomer herself acquired a sackful from a stockbroker because she fancied using them as wallpaper when business improved. Lucius was furious on discovering she had paid the dealer as much as $250 for them, and forced him to refund the money, claiming that his wife had been swindled.

Despite its unpropitious reopening, the Waldorf-Astoria slowly made headway. The cuisine and restaurant service could not be faulted, thanks to the ability of Oscar's successor as *maître d'hôtel*, C. C. Philippe, and the enjoyment of the clientèle was heightened by the fine music provided.

Albert Morris Bagby, that popular educational entertainer and presenter of morning musicales in the old hotel, continued to do so in the new. His reign, in fact, lasted for nearly forty years and he always provided superb programmes. In 1938, for example, the artists included Kirsten Flagstad, Lotte Lehmann, Lily Pons, Richard Crooks and Lauritz Melchior. Bagby went to infinite pains to please his audiences, and would pay the ticket-takers at the Met to let him know where those who frequented it liked to sit, so that he could try and seat them in similar locations.

Waldorf-Astoria II's main attraction was its Starlight Roof restaurant which eventually became extremely popular with the new café-society, though in the early days there were times when Jack Benny and his orchestra outnumbered the guests staying in the hotel.

The Wall Street crash had at least brought to the fore those with sharp wits and resourcefulness, who found ways of surviving. Harry Sell, editor of *Harper's Bazaar*, refused to be depressed when most of the advertising space reserved in the magazine's pages was cancelled by insolvent firms: he had been responsible for running the entertainment side of the Hearst organization, and was a past master of publicity stunts – such as enlivening pompous banquets by following some gastronomic speciality with hot dogs brought in by singing Italian street-vendors, or suddenly surrounding the diners with shrieking bands of gypsies brandishing deafening tambourines, whom, to ensure good luck, he would reward for their efforts with gold coins. Sell also ran his own private advertising agency, and he now used it to exploit his ingenious scheme for bringing back customers to the languishing Waldorf-Astoria. He enlisted well-dressed and attractive but impoverished young people, who were deft dancers, to act as partners to the lonely rich and to persuade them to spend lavishly on food and drink. Harry Sell kept a close watch on these gigolos and gigolettes, and those who brought in the most cash this way were given further grooming, and then exercised their talents among widows and the divorced on the great luxury liners.

Lucius Boomer in the early 1930s also signed an agreement with MCA to provide the artists and bands for the Empire Room, the Peacock Lounge, the Sert Room, and the Starlight Roof, and it was there that most of the famous stars of American popular music first started. In time the new hotel attracted some of these to make their homes in a separate section called The Towers, which consisted of 116 private apartments. In one of these, Cole Porter, during a long tenancy, composed many of his best songs.

★
Rector's

★

An electric sign representing a griffin hung outside a long, low, yellow building on the corner of 44th St and Broadway which was the first restaurant in the United States to have an orchestra for dancing during meals. Its extrovert owner, Charles Rector, started earning his living by driving a horsecart on the Second Avenue line. Moving to Chicago, he took over a squalid bar which he transformed with his drive and hearty good humour into a sea-food goldmine; and with the profits from this he opened his New York venture on 23 September 1899. Customers entered through a revolving door, never before used in an American restaurant. As a result, it was taken over by the neighbourhood's youth who for hours prevented any customers penetrating inside: rumour had it that some 5,000 of the youths took part. At last a solitary elderly man went through, having distracted the whirligig fans' attention away from their sport by scattering a few coins.

Rector's first guest was the Wall Street financier George A. Kessler who six years later at the Savoy in London held the famous Gondola Dinner to celebrate the King's birthday. As he entered the dining-room, Charles Rector signalled to the leader of the Russian symphony orchestra which he had engaged to welcome him with music.

The new restaurant was to become the favourite eating-place of some of Broadway's most colourful characters, and of those who wanted to enjoy themselves free of the curbs of convention. With completely mirrored walls reflecting the imposing crystal chandeliers and the opulent gold-and-green decorative scheme, Rector's looked much larger than it actually was. The hundred tables downstairs were reserved for regulars and celebrities, while lesser mortals could be accommodated at some seventy or so tables on the first floor. There were also four private dining-rooms. It was considered extremely daring for a lady from high society to be seen at Rector's. Elaborate precautions were usually taken to avoid recognition: if supping there after the theatre, she would go home first, change her gown for one that was not décolleté, put on her shadiest hat, and insist on her admirer reserving a table in as inconspicuous a position as possible.

Many like to boast to acquaintances and friends that they have eaten at fashionable restaurants, and to convince the sceptical of the truth of such claims they may produce an ashtray or a spoon which the kind owner or *maître d'hôtel* 'gave' them. As a result of this craze, Rector's lost on average every year 2,000 pieces of silverware bearing its griffin crest. The worst case of souvenir-hunting occurred when a coffee-percolator weighing about 8 lb and costing $75 was smuggled out by a lady diner under the $8,000-worth of ermine in which she was enveloped. Shortly afterwards people on Broadway were startled to see a lady and a gentleman jump out of a blazing two-wheeler hansom cab. She had forgotten to extinguish the heater of the percolator. The cabman sued her for the damage caused him; Rector's hardly recognized their ravaged property; while the fur was scorched bald. At least its owner was not roasted.

Rector's first head chef was the stout, heavy-eating and -drinking Emil Hederer, pride of the Waldorf, whom Charles Rector had tempted away by paying him $7,000 a year. He was famed for his 'Terrapin à la Maryland'. Already in his sixties, he eventually proved too temperamental and departed, to be succeeded by the young chief sauce cook, Charles Perraudin, who had been lured away from Delmonico's. Rival restaurateurs were acidly to accuse him of making his red, brown and purple sauces for meats so rich that they tinted the over-stuffed patrons' faces with the same colours.

A thin customer, and one of the oddest, for whom Rector's imported Burgundy-bred snails, was Dan Daly, Edna May's co-star from *The Belle of New York*. He had always eaten and drunk in moderation, only having his main meal after midnight, when suddenly he changed to a snails-only diet which he washed down with champagne. After doing this for two years, he quietly expired.

The restaurant's fame was spread far and wide by Nat Wills' song in Flo Ziegfeld's first *Follies* – 'If A Table In Rector's Could Talk'. Wills' wife rode a white horse bareback in a circus, now turning double somersaults, now leaping through a paper hoop. Once they had a furious quarrel and she threw him right through the closed dressing-room door. He rubbed his head and said sadly: 'I should have married the horse.'

Often the stars from Broadway's musical comedies enchanted others supping after the show by singing popular numbers. Victor Herbert himself would sit at the piano and accompany William Pruette as he shook the place with his deep bass declaring: 'I Want What I Want When I Want It' from the genial composer's *Mlle Modiste*, and the supper crowd would join in the chorus, emphasizing the 'wants' by banging their fists on the tables. Sometimes Herbert brought with him Fritzi Scheff, the soprano whom he had coaxed away from the Met to play a snare drum and sing entrancingly 'Kiss Me Again' in the same operetta. Herbert was so genuinely liked by the orchestra that they played a medley of melodies from his works whenever he came in. (Much-married male stars, on arrival with a new bride, would be greeted by 'The Minstrel Boy To The War Has Gone'.)

It was over dinner at Rector's that Flo Ziegfeld suggested to vaudeville comedian Charles Evan Evans that they should turn into a musical *A Parlor Match*, the longest running play in the history of the American stage until then. The suggestion proved to be the first step towards fame and fortune for Flo, who already had assembled a collection of catchy numbers including 'Daisy Bell' which he sang in his near falsetto to Evans – and found those at neighbouring tables joining him in the irresistible refrain, '*Daisy, Daisy, give me your answer, do*'.

The new partners left for Europe in search of the right actress to play Lucille in the musical, and at London's Palace Theatre they found her: bewitching Anna Held with her opalescent eyes, eighteen-inch waist, faultless timing of sexy shrugs and wriggles, and delightful, tantalizing laugh. 'Come and Play With Me', she invited and that was what the men at Rector's would like to have done the night Flo Ziegfeld first brought her there for supper. An eye-witness wrote: 'Poised, while a gypsy violinist established himself at the train of her dress, Miss Anna Held swept into the room – the violinist serenading her softly – a vision in yellow crêpe de Chine trimmed with poppies in full bloom, her wide eyes an open invitation to French frivolity.' The occasion was after her triumph in the première of *Papa's Wife*, singing, 'I Just Can't Make My Eyes Behave'.

Sales of milk soared in New York, thanks to Anna, and some male admirers even started asking for glasses of milk instead of champagne when dining at Rector's. For every afternoon at the Netherlands Hotel her maid would dissolve starch in the bathwater and Anna would lie in this for two hours because she believed that it maintained her skin's milky whiteness. When Ziegfeld discovered this, he visited a dairyman, H. R. Wallace, and secretly arranged that he would deliver daily a churn of milk at the hotel labelled: 'For Miss Anna Held'. After a week, Ziegfeld would abruptly cancel the order, and Wallace would sue them on the grounds that there had been a firm commitment to take 400 gallons over a period of three weeks. Invaluable front-page publicity would then be gained for Anna, with the disclosure that she took milk baths.

All went as planned; even the *New York Times* was taken in and reported: 'Mr John Anderson, a Brooklyn lawyer, has been instructed to sue Mr Ziegfeld and Miss Held for $64 in unpaid milk bills.' The defendants' representative was quoted later as saying: 'The matter will be settled out of court, as milk baths are too peculiar to be discussed in public.' Nevertheless, the press were invited to interview Anna immersed in a bath of real milk, on which occasion she told them: 'The milk Mr Wallace delivered was not fresh. This milk is much better.' And Ziegfeld added: 'His cows must have been milked days before, and by the time she got it, the milk was sour.' 'It was – oh – *horrible!*' Anna cried when later, on the stage of the Academy of Music in full view of a packed audience, a writ was served on her. 'A milk bath should be very grateful and refreshing. It is for the skin, to benefit the skin. Wasn't it Marie Antoinette who used to bathe in milk? But this milk was *cream!*'

Wallace was furious when he heard his milk being thus denigrated, there having been no suggestion that poor quality should be given as the reason for breaking the contract. He summoned the press to his dairy and exposed Ziegfeld as a hoaxer.

Rector's described as 'the best twenty-five customers we ever had' a man whom others eulogized as 'Broadway's master of revels', its 'premier angel' and its 'greatest host' – the son of an Irish saloon-keeper, who through a flair for business and speculation became a dollar multi-millionaire. Weighing eighteen stone, Diamond Jim Brady had three chins, beneath which started his stomach, estimated as being six times the normal size. Purple-faced and piggy-eyed, he had a smile that made one forget his ugliness, it was so full of bonhomie and zest for life. One's attention, too, was inevitably attracted to his blaze of diamonds. He had thirty matching sets made up from over 20,000 stones, as well as some 6,000 rubies and sapphires. Arrayed every day in one or other of these, he resembled (as a wit observed) 'an excursion steamer at midnight'. He ordered his suits by the dozen, and once a year would give away all his clothes and household goods and embark on a shopping spree.

Twelve-course dinners were customary in Brady's day, and he would very often put away three extra helpings of each main dish, finishing with a 12-egg soufflé. Another frequenter of Rector's, Wilson Mizner, said he noticed that Jim liked his oysters 'sprinkled with clams' and his steaks 'smothered in veal cutlets'. Strangers often bet on whether or not he would be carried out feet first, as they watched the disappearance of four dozen Lynnhaven extra-large oysters, specially shipped daily for him from Baltimore, followed by the restaurant's famed Lobster American (with two crustaceans instead of the usual one), and a dozen hard-shelled crabs – after which he was ready for his main dishes.

'Whenever I sit down to a meal,' Brady once revealed, 'I always make it a point to leave just four inches between my

James Buchanan Brady – 'Diamond Jim' – the American
multi-millionaire with a passion for jewels, for musical
comedies and food

stummick and the edge of the table. And then when I can feel
'em rubbin' together pretty hard, I know I've had enough.'

Brady was practically a teetotaller, and the first thing he
would order on arriving at about 7.30 p.m. at Rector's was
freshly squeezed orange juice, of which he drank a gallon before

beginning to eat. This was followed by another three gallons during the course of the meal. Some instinct must have told him that this would counteract any harmful effects from over-eating, for later medical opinion reached the same conclusion.

On nights when he went to the theatre, Diamond Jim ate at Rector's after the show. His favourite pastime was going to the premières of musical comedies, always booking seats in the centre of the front row and refusing to sit elsewhere. It was the era of huge hats for women, and he declared: 'I'll be damned if I'm gonna pay my good money to sit and look at a lot of stuffed birds and laces.' His verdict was anxiously awaited by the cast and the backers. Flo Ziegfeld said: 'If Diamond Jim went to sleep before the first act was over, failure was a sure bet. If he stayed awake for two acts, they knew there were chances for a fair run. If he stayed awake for three acts and was still interested at the fall of the curtain, success was sure.'

Following a trip to Paris, Brady returned raving about the sauce served with the sole at the Café de Marguéry. Charles Rector's son George, after working for two years in their own kitchens, had gone to Cornell to study law and was about to graduate. Despite this, so as to please Diamond Jim, father sent the youth to Paris with orders not to return until he had mastered the art of making this sauce. First, George served as an apprentice cook at the Café de Paris under the most testing conditions, for eight months. If croûtons were not at the proper temperature, consommé of the correct consistency, even knives and forks not perfectly laid out, one was demoted to the ignominious rank of 'omnibus' and forced to carry the heaviest dishes for the waiters.

Promoted at last to the status of a journeyman waiter, George one day served a Russian aristocrat with cèpes and sauce Bordelaise, and this epicure, on tasting the sauce, declared with disgust that it was impossible for him to swallow such stuff. His ultra-sensitive palate had detected George's blunder in adding the sweet oil before the butter, for which gaffe he was reduced to 'bus boy for a month.

In due course George moved on to the Café de Marguéry,

where he spent sixty days learning the art of making the sauce that Diamond Jim rated so highly. Then he submitted himself to a practical test before a jury of seven master-chefs and won their unanimous approval. As a reward he was sent to the Palais des Champs Elysées to prepare the sauce for a dinner in honour of King Oscar of Sweden, but the King asked for *Filet Mignon Hederer* instead. George knew the recipe, as Hederer was now his father's master-chef, and acquitted himself so admirably that he was decorated by the French Government and made an honorary member of the Société des Cuisiniers de Paris, the first American to have his culinary skill so acknowledged.

George then sent his father a cable to say he was sailing for New York, and once on board ship obtained permission from the steward to use the kitchen, where he made the sauce again and again so as to perfect his expertise. Brady and Charles Rector, together with the restaurant's Russian orchestra playing welcoming music, were awaiting him at the dock. 'Have you got the sauce?' bellowed through a megaphone Diamond Jim, who was wearing his dazzling 'Transportation Set'. This consisted of large diamonds mounted in platinum shaped as bicycles, automobiles, railroad engines, and Pullman cars, for shirt and vest studs, and a diamond aeroplane in his lapel buttonhole.

They rushed George uptown and he began making preparations for the dinner to be given that night. At eight o'clock a group of *bons vivants* sat down at a big table: Victor Herbert, Sam Shubert and his show-business rivals Klaw and Erlanger, Dan Reid the tin-plate king, Marshall Field, Adolphus Busch, Alfred Henry Lewis of Wolfville fame, as well as Brady himself. It was midnight when George left the kitchen to be congratulated. Jim said: 'That sole was marvellous. I've had nine helpings and even right now if you poured some of the sauce over a Turkish towel, I believe I could eat all of it.' (George Rector's recipe for *Sole Marguéry* can be found on page 213).

Tubby and jovial George Rector himself was to say of the man who paid him such a tribute: 'Don't let anyone ever tell you that he didn't know all there was to know about food. He was the greatest gourmet of his time.' As for most of the other customers, George admitted that Rector's menu, like that of Sherry's and Delmonico's, was based more on the vanity than the palate of their diners. One lady, because strawberries were so expensive and had to be imported from Spain, ordered some in January to make those in her vicinity jealous. But she would merely hold one up in the air on a fork and take an occasional nibble; the rest she sent back to be kept in the ice-box, and like that they lasted for a month.

George Rector claimed in his reminiscences, that for a quarter of a century Rector's was 'the centre of the web spun by the benevolent spider of Manhattan in its effort to snare the genius, ability, and beauty of America'. Actually that reign nearly ended in the twelfth year of the restaurant's existence. In 1911, becoming over-ambitious, father and son built the Hotel Rector with 250 bedrooms as well as a restaurant. This took a year, during which time Rector's was closed and customers fell into the habit of patronizing a number of attractive new restaurants like the Café de l'Opéra, Churchill's, Murray's and Shanley's. When the new hotel opened, not only did the old clientèle not flow back, but the production of a bedroom farce, *The Girl From Rector's*, gave the false impression that the hotel was already a hotbed of vice. For three months no one would stay there, and they were losing $1,000 daily.

The outlook was grim when one day George M. Cohan, famous composer of such 'hits' as 'Give My Regards To Broadway', 'Yankee Doodle Dandy', and '[Mary Is] A Grand Old Name', came in. 'Where is the crowd?' he asked on seeing the empty restaurant. Over dinner the two Rectors told him, and he rallied to their support, saying, 'I'm going to live in your hotel and so are my friends. I'm going to eat in your restaurant again, and so are my pals. Get me a suite of rooms on the second floor facing Broadway. I'm going to live there by the year.'

Cohan kept his promise, and within a week all the bedrooms were let. For five years the Hotel Rector survived, but it failed to make enough profit to pay the interest on the mortgage owed to the builders, who in the end seized the property. Charles Rector died of grief within the year.

The new craze of ragtime sweeping the country was causing a revolution not only in dancing but also in eating habits. The itch to bunny-hug, kangaroo dip, crab step, camel- or fish-walk, turkey- or fox-trot, made enthusiasts jump up and gyrate frenziedly between courses. The need to earn a living led to George Rector's attempt to cater for this new market, and in partnership with two men he started a restaurant at 48th St and Broadway. 'It was more like a madhouse,' he wrote later. Some 1,500 people each paid a cover charge of $1, and were all of a class absolutely different from any he had ever met. He described in his reminiscences how all they wanted was to dance, which they tried to do at the same time on a floor measuring thirty feet by twenty feet. The diners would drop their knives and forks and stampede for this postage-stamp the minute the orchestra, famous for its endurance and volume, began playing. The first year's profits paid off the partners' original investment of $200,000 and left them another $100,000. This enabled them to engage four orchestras playing in relays and sounding 'like mechanics repairing a locomotive'.

George found that nobody really came in to dine, so most of the time the chefs were out on the dance-floor with the customers, and the waiters 'hugged' and 'trotted' with the women employees. Gourmet customers from the old days complained to him that jazz was ruining the art of dining, that nobody could eat a quiet luncheon 'in a boiler factory' and it was impossible to carry on a conversation 'in the Tower of Babel'. There was a time when they had dined to 'the digestive lubrication of soft string music' but in the new Rector's the only things 'stringy' were the steaks and chops. 'The worse we grew,' George adds, 'the bigger crowds we drew. Our waiters were renowned for their intelligent insults and our captains for their dexterity in hustling indignant diners to the doors . . . Owing to the terrific noise, we had no use for mezzo-sopranos trained on bird-seed. Our soloists were picked out for their ability to run the hay scales and register on seismographs . . . Sometimes I felt twinges of conscience when I looked around at the idiotic panorama, but I forgot them when I checked up my share of the plunder.' And to anyone planning a first visit and wanting to know how to dress, his wry advice would be, 'The most important article of evening clothing is the ear-muff.'

One old patron, however, kept up with the times – Diamond Jim. Now in his late fifties, he took dancing lessons, practised tirelessly, excelled at the turkey-trot and the tango, and lived on the dance floors of all the roof restaurants and cabarets that were continually opening to cater for the craze – places such as Manhattan's first night-club, Lee Shubert's Palais de Danse, Castles-in-the-Air, and William Morris's Jardin de Danse. Like everyone else, Diamond Jim never stayed in one place but moved on, sometimes visiting as many as four of his haunts before retiring. No one was more popular than he with the other addicts. The moment the orchestra started, Brady occupied what came to be regarded as his exclusive territory, the middle of the floor, and he remained there, humming happily and stroking his partner's back in time to the music. Up to a dozen attractive girls, all hired for the evening and expert dancers, accompanied him, for he was continually on the floor and as one flagged another took over. They were allowed to eat as much food as they liked and were paid $25 for their services. Each one was lent a fur coat for the evening only, so as to be suitably glamorously wrapped, but it had to be surrendered before going home. His close association with the Dolly Sisters began in that way.

It was war-time Prohibition that finally ended the third Rector's, and on New Year's Day 1919, exactly twenty years after the first Rector's had opened its doors, the famous electric griffin outside was switched off for ever.

Millions of Americans who had never set foot inside Rector's were familiar with its name through mention of it not only in the press but on the stage and in popular songs. Comedians jested: 'I told my secretary that I once found a valuable pearl in an oyster, and she replied: "That's nothing. I got a diamond from a lobster in Rector's last night."' And in David Belasco's long-running play, *The Easiest Way*, the final curtain line from Frances Starr to the man she is walking out on, goes: 'You go to hell. I am going to Rector's.'

―――――――――――――― ★ ――――――――――――――
'The Gastronomic Symposium
of All Nations'
―――――――――――――― ★ ――――――――――――――

Few people attending concerts in the Royal Albert Hall are likely to know that it stands on the site once occupied by the Gastronomic Symposium of All Nations, a collection of some forty extraordinary restaurants, cafés and bars which was the brainchild of Alexis Soyer, the celebrated chef of the Reform Club and probably the most musical of the great pioneers of the gastronomic art. Starting work at the age of twelve at Chez Grignon's, a Mecca for gourmets in Paris, Soyer in five years had risen to being in charge of a dozen cooks at the Maison Douix in the Boulevard des Italiens.

Having a good ear and an attractive tenor voice, Soyer nursed the ambition of going on the stage, and when he was off duty he spent most of his evenings at the Paris Opéra. Leaving there, he would make his way conspiratorially to some café in a back street and eat fried fish, which he preferred to anything else. It was with difficulty that his brother Philippe restrained him from trying his luck as an actor, and he made up for this by wearing startlingly bizarre clothes all his life, and by his exhibitionist behaviour.

Soyer was also a balletomane who admired Fanny Cerrito and created a dish in her honour. Later, he devised the choreography for a ballet, *La Fille de l'Orage*, but it proved so complicated that it was never performed.

In 1830 he became second chef to the French Foreign Minister, and when the Revolution broke out on 26 July that year the mob broke into the Foreign Office and shot two under-cooks before his very eyes. The others fled, abandoning Soyer to his fate. Desperately, and with all the feeling he could muster, he burst into the *Marseillaise*, and instead of killing him the rioters cheered and bore him shoulder-high as their singing mascot through the streets of Paris. So music saved his life, as it had saved Brillat-Savarin's during the French Revolution.

With the change of government, Alexis Soyer left Paris for London, where he eventually became the chef of the new Reform Club in Pall Mall and designed its kitchens, which were regarded as the finest in the world. They were 'white as a young bride', wrote the London correspondent of the *Courrier de l'Europe*. 'All-powerful steam . . . diffuses a uniform heat to large rows of dishes, warms the metal plates, upon which are disposed the dishes that have been called for and that are waiting above, it operates the spits, draws the water, carries up the coal, and moves the plate like an intelligent and tireless servant. Around one water boils, stewpans bubble, and a few steps further on is a moveable furnace, before which meat is roasted. Here are sauces, gravies, broths, etc., and in the distance are dutch ovens, marble mortars, lighted stoves, iced metal plates for fish, and compartments for vegetables, fruits, roots and spices . . . The order of their arrangement is so perfect, their distribution as a whole, and in their bearings to one another, all are so intelligently integrated, that you need the aid of a guide fully to appreciate their merits.'

Every afternoon visitors were allowed to inspect the kitchens, 'the cleanliness of which would shame many a drawing-room'. The more important guests were shown round by Soyer himself, who thoroughly enjoyed doing so – for, as he said, 'Publicity is like the air we breathe: if we have it not, we die.' The tribute that must have pleased him most was when *The Globe* newspaper declared: 'The impression grows on us that the man of his age is neither Sir Robert Peel, nor Lord John Russell, nor even Ibrahim Pasha, but Alexis Soyer.'

Soyer certainly deserved this praise. All who worked for him were far better treated and paid than elsewhere in those times. He was also deeply concerned about the plight of the poor and opened soup-kitchens for them in London, and in Dublin where, owing to the failure of the potato crop, thousands of Irish were dying of starvation.

After twelve years Soyer left the Reform Club and concentrated on organizing important banquets and indulging his taste for imposing theatrical effects. In 1850, for the annual dinner of the Royal Agricultural Society in Exeter, he arranged an open-air banquet the highlight of which was the roasting of a 530-lb ox by gas – the first time this had been done. The 'Saddleback and Baron of Beef à la Magna Carta' was then carried through the streets by eight men, accompanied by a band playing 'The Roast Beef of Old England'. That same year on 25 October he mounted a banquet in York for all the mayors of the United Kingdom. Prince Albert was the guest of honour, and before him was set the most costly and showy dish Soyer ever contrived, which he called *L'Extravagance Culinaire à l'Alderman* or *The Hundred-Guinea Dish* (that being his estimate of its value). He informed the press that it had been prepared from choice morsels selected from all the birds mentioned in the general bill of fare, while the garniture consisted of cocks' combs, truffles, mushrooms, crawfish, olives, asparagus, croustades, sweetbreads, *quenelles de volailles*, green mangoes, and a new sauce whose recipe he must keep secret.

That banquet helped to gather support for Prince Albert's pet project, the Great Exhibition to be held the following year in Hyde Park. Soyer was not interested in catering for visitors to the Crystal Palace because of various restrictions there, including a ban on the sale of alcoholic drinks. Two hundred yards from its entrance, however, stood elegant Gore House surrounded by its beautiful gardens; it had been the much-admired home of the celebrated hostess Lady Blessington until, in 1849, she had retired to Paris to avoid arrest for debt. Her creditors had sold the contents of the house, and in 1851 it could be rented for a £100 a month. Borrowing the necessary money, Soyer leased the place for six months and, with the assistance of writer George Augustus Sala, proceeded to transform it into the Gastronomic Symposium of All Nations.

Sala's role was supposed to be that of interior decorator, but Soyer, with inexhaustible enthusiasm, took complete charge. He supervised the designing, the carpenters, and the plumbers. Ignoring the problem of how he was going to settle the bills, he engaged hundreds of workmen and ordered luxurious fittings and furnishings. He intended that the Symposium should put the Crystal Palace in the shade.

Sala relates in his reminiscences how Soyer made him paint on the grand staircase 'a panorama containing every celebrity that could be crowded in. They were all portrayed rushing up the stairs on the backs of every conceivable animal, and on foot; everyone who Soyer could think of, from Napoleon to Ali Baba, from Dickens to mobs of Indians and savages, all proceeding pell-mell up the stairs in one mad rush. He insisted that this panoramic rubbish be called the Grand *Macédoine* of all Nations.'

Lady Blessington and her son-in-law, the Comte d'Orsay, forced exiles in Paris, read with horrified amazement the newspaper accounts of how the rooms of Gore House had been converted into cafés and restaurants bearing such names as the Blessington Temple of the Muses, Cupid's Delight, the Bower of Ariadne, the Dungeon of Mystery, Flora's Retreat, the Hall of Architectural Wonders, the Transatlantic Passage, the Peruvian Forest, the Gallic Pavilion, the Washington Refreshment Room, Soyer's Colossal Offering to Amphitrite, the Gigantic Encampment of all Nations, the Glittering Rocaille of Eternal Snows, Hebe's Mistake, the Ariel Orchestra, the Emerald Pyramids of Morning Dew, the Impenetrable Grotto of Ondine, *L'Avenue des Amours*, the Gypsy Dell, the Baronial Hall, the Show of Gems, the Night of the Stars, the Grand Banqueting Bridge, the Celestial Hall of the Golden Lilies, and so on.

An enormous pavilion, the Gigantic Encampment of all Nations, was erected in the grounds, and had a table over 300 feet long, where up to 1,500 people could sit together and dine, thus (according to the guide to the Symposium) being able to enjoy the conviviality of a public banquet. Americans might

The 'Gastronomic Symposium of All Nations', Gore
House, Kensington, 1851. In the gardens can be seen
(centre) the Impenetrable Grotto of Ondine

buy food and drink which was the equivalent of anything back
home, in the Transatlantic Passage or the Washington Refreshment Room. In fact, Soyer claimed that most national dishes
were available in his catering complex.

In addition to that grand staircase panorama, Sala relates that
he was kept busy painting the walls everywhere 'with a gro-
tesque nightmare of portraits of people I have never seen, and
hundreds more upon whom I have never set eyes, save in the
print shops, till I saw the originals grinning, or scowling, or
planted in blank amazement before all the pictorial libels on the
wall'.

In mid-April, well-known people were invited by Soyer to
make conducted tours of the Symposium before the general
public. Wellington, it seems, was fascinated and paid three

visits. Unfortunately there is no record of his impressions. Disraeli, the Russian Ambassador, and the ballerina, Fanny Cerrito, also came. The latter, for whom Soyer had created his unproduced ballet, was proudly dined and wined by him in a restaurant named after it, *La Vestibule de la Fille de l'Orage*, the walls of which Sala, at his direction, had adorned with imaginary scenes of Fanny, voluptuously posed, executing her famed revolving bounds and flying leaps in the ballet. He depicted her as much slimmer than she was in real life, for, as a critic wrote, owing to her love of fine food, her figure would be 'too redundant were it not for its extreme flexibility and abandon'.

The press were also entertained by Soyer, and with such attention that they rewarded him with favourable accounts of everything. Only *Punch* censured him for having 'glaringly defaced Gore House'. However good his palate was, the magazine disputed the quality of his taste.

'Finally,' Sala wrote later, 'having engaged an army of pages, cooks, scullions and waiters, barmaids and clerks of the kitchen, we opened this monstrous place on the first of May, and bade all the World to come and dine at Soyer's Symposium.' The public flocked there in large numbers. The food and service did not live up to their expectations and there were many complaints: it was quite impossible, of course, with such a plethora of cafés and restaurants and such a variety of menus, for Soyer to keep a close watch on all the cooking. Always optimistic and full of new ideas, he was busy marketing bottled sauces, as well as inventing ingenious kitchen utensils of which he himself, ever eager to keep in the public eye, would demonstrate the uses.

When the Great Exhibition closed, Soyer remained at Gore House providing facilities for private parties and society dinners. At some of these he arranged for the flamboyant conductor, Jullien, and his orchestra to play, and this led to their agreeing to form a partnership and build a music hall at Gore House. Application for a licence was made and granted. Then a magistrate, paying a surprise visit of inspection, happened to arrive on an evening when a vicar had brought some 200 of his parishioners to dine at the Symposium. Afterwards they joined 500 or so other visitors in frequenting the bars and dancing polkas, quadrilles, and waltzes to the music of that showman Jullien's lively orchestra. The magistrate was shocked, and

Soyer's Sauce: an advertisement showing the chef Alexis Soyer in the centre of the bottle's label

declared that he had never come across 'a more dissipated or dangerous place for the morals of young people'. It disgraced the neighbourhood, he said.

Soyer was extremely upset when he heard about this and, valuing above all his reputation, he closed the Symposium forthwith. Parliament had refused to supply funds for setting up and running the Great Exhibition, so its originator, Prince Albert, had been obliged to find the finance from private sources. To his delight, the enterprise made a large profit, and in 1852 some of that money was used to buy Gore House and its 21-acre grounds. The original intention of building a new National Gallery on the site was not pursued, and the Royal Albert Hall was erected there instead. That music-lover, Alexis Soyer, whose unfulfilled ambition was to be a great actor or singer, would have approved.

The Royal Albert Hall in its long life has been used for many purposes, including those to do with food. In 1907 it was the scene of a dinner given to the Premiers attending the Colonial Conference, when no fewer than 1,600 people sat down to what was believed to be the biggest banquet ever held in London. The records show that 2¼ tons of beef were used to make the soup, which was followed by 200 whole salmon, 2,500 quails, 25,000 stalks of asparagus, and 600 lbs of strawberries. Some 500 cooks and waiters prepared and served all this. As for drink, 1,400 bottles of champagne and 1,500 of hock were soon emptied, as well as the contents of 300 bottles of cognac and the same of chartreuse and whisky, plus 500 of crème de menthe. The whole cost was £4,000.

More recently, in 1983, the Design and Art Directors' Association held their 21st anniversary party in the Albert Hall. Under the heading, 'Masterpiece – or just a *chef d'oeuf*' the *Sunday Times* wrote that the vast memorial to Queen Victoria's consort had witnessed some strange events, 'but last Thursday saw one of the strangest – the ceremonial poaching of 2,500 eggs'. This was achieved by three highly qualified chefs, four or five basins with water and vinegar, 'and several hours', said Albert Roux, proprietor of *Le Gavroche* restaurant, who was in charge, assisted by a further twenty-one chefs and 320 waitresses.

--- ★ ---

Boulestin's

--- ★ ---

The great London chefs of the years between the First and Second World Wars were François Latry of the Savoy and Eugène Herbodeau of the Ritz, but – as Gregory Houston Bowden wrote in *British Gastronomy* – 'when one is seeking to find the person who had the greatest influence on the post-war revival of gastronomy and indeed throughout the whole inter-war period, the award must surely go to one who, in the first instance, was more a journalist and interior decorator than a chef, Marcel Boulestin.'

Boulestin was interested in music from childhood, learnt to play the piano and became music critic for *Le Mercure Musical* in Paris. In the early 1920s he came to London and tried unsuccessfully to earn his living as an interior decorator. To survive, he began giving French lessons and cooking for well-to-do people's dinner-parties, and he gained such a reputation that Heinemann commissioned him to write his *Simple French Cooking for English Homes*. This was so well received that in May 1925, with Robin Adair as partner, he opened the Restaurant Français in Leicester Square with Bigorre from Paillard's as chef. It proved a perfect combination of talent, for Bigorre supplied the practical experience which the other two did not have, and yet was completely co-operative. Impressed by Boulestin's outstandingly original recipes, he delighted in using them, and the new venture attracted a discerning clientèle right from the start. It was different, too, from other small restaurants in that it offered *à la carte* eating instead of *table d'hôte*.

It was soon clear that the converted shop in Leicester Square was too small and a few months later, in November, a move was made to premises at 25 Southampton Street which they named the Restaurant Boulestin. Seven chefs and a salad- and coffee-maker catered for up to eighty people. The kitchen was equipped with a coal range and charcoal grills because Boulestin maintained that cooking in this fashion was essential for *haute cuisine*.

Gourmets now flocked to Boulestin's. Cecil Beaton, in his diary for August 1928, records being invited with Rex Whistler to dine there and describes it as 'the prettiest restaurant in London, with its deep yellow varnished walls, cloudy mirrors and Dufy-designed silks'. They sat on banquettes and 'in the most leisurely and epicurean manner enjoyed Osbert's talk, the cheese sauces and wines'.

Being but a short walk from the Royal Opera House, Boulestin's swiftly drew regular diners from the world of music – conductors like Furtwängler and Beecham, singers like Conchita Supervia, Kirsten Flagstad, Frida Leider, and Lauritz Melchior whose vocal magic rendered audiences oblivious of his bulky figure, so that they accepted him as the young Siegfried. Authors like Lord Derwent and Francis Toye, who were experts on Rossini, also dined there, and such patrons of the opera as the Courtaulds.

When there were performances of *The Ring*, all the tables would be booked weeks ahead and extra staff engaged. Though the interval was usually only one hour long, the Wagner buffs hurrying in to dine after the first act of *Das Rheingold*, *Die Walküre*, *Siegfried*, or *Götterdämmerung* were all expeditiously served without fuss or any deterioration of cooking standards. In the restaurant's main room there was a curtained recess where Boulestin, inspired by Bayreuth, concealed an Opera House trumpeter; ten minutes before the performance resumed, the trumpeter played a piece from the work being presented, as a signal that it was time to return to the Royal Opera House. The first time that conversation was interrupted in this way, it so surprised the diners that they applauded spontaneously. The trumpeter was delighted and told Boulestin

[86]

PETIT CONCERT GASTRONOMIQUE

BOULESTIN

**Restaurant francais
25, Southampton Street
Covent Garden, W.C.2**

PROGRAMME

Analytical notes by X. M. Boulestin, late musical critic to Le Mercure Musical and S.I.M. (Société Internationale de Musique).

LE MARCHÉ (A. Samain)   H. Villa Lobos

A brilliant description of the potential dishes the market can supply. In this case, to be considered as an apéritif-prelude, destined, like all preludes, to put the listeners in the right state of mind.

DIE FORELLE (Schubart)   Franz Schubert

The trout is a very good theme for many variations: *au bleu, meunière, meunière* with a banana fried in the same butter (*scherzando*), grilled and with melted butter, *cold en gelée*, treated with dry white wine and cream (this *legato* treatment being one of the best) are but different aspects of the same charming idea.

LA CARPE (G. Apollinaire)   F. Poulenc

Boiled river fish is not to be despised, but it must be cooked in a carefully made *court bouillon*, well flavoured with wine, onion, bouquet, coarsely broken pepper and aromatic herbs. The carp is often served in the country around Nantes with a special sauce called "*beurre blanc*" or stuffed and baked. The roes are delicious.

LA PINTADE (J. RENARD)   M. Ravel

The flesh of the guinea-fowl being of a dry nature, it is advisable to give this bird a rich and savoury accompaniment. It is particularly good roasted wrapped in bacon, often basted, then, *flambée* with brandy and served with *croûtons* well spread with *foie gras*.

LES PETITS CANARDS (ROSEMONDE GÉRARD)
E. Chabrier

Take a young duck and put it in a casserole with a good piece of butter. Start it on the stove and finish it in the oven, when you add a sauce made of roux to which is added tomato purée, white wine, consommé and a bouquet. Half-way through, add button onions and small turnips, simmer gently till the duck is cooked. Skim off the fat and serve very hot.

LA POULE NOIRE (LISE HIRTZ)   G. Auric

The *poule au pot* no doubt was known even in the Middle Ages, but it made its first official appearance in History the day that Henri IV popularized it throughout France; it is doubtful if the garlic from Béarn which the stuffing certainly contained was appreciated above the Loire. Dinner in those days took place at about ten o'clock in the morning (solar time). The hours have changed: the dish has remained.

UNE PETITE POMME (LISE HIRTZ)   G. Auric

Apples are an important item in a fruitarian menu. Cooked, they are at their best, as a marmalade, or fried and flavoured with cinnamon and served with whipped cream.

Sung by MADAME SOPHIE WYSS

CHANSONS À LA CHARCUTIÈRE
(FRANC-NOHAIN)   C. Terrasse

(*a*) Du pays Tourangeau
(*b*) Malheureuse Adèle

Sung *by* MADAME ALICE DELYSIA

(a) *Du pays Tourangeau.*

1

Du pays tourangeau
La jeune châtelaine
Garnit de blanche laine
Son agile fuseau;
C'est Yette qu'on l'appelle,
Et Yette est la plus belle.
  A tourné pour se voir
  Les yeux vers son miroir
  Rajuste sa cornette
  Et se voit si proprette
  Dedans ses beaux atours,
  Se fait une risette
Ris, Yette, ris Yette de Tours.

2

Un chant mélodieux
Chante sous sa fenêtre
Et puis voici paraître
Gentil page aux doux yeux
Lui conte sa tristesse
Amoureuse détresse:
  Si tu ne m'aimes pas
  Pour moi c'est le trépas.
  Mais point n'inquiète
  La cruelle coquette,
  Et rit de son discours.
  Il s'est coupé la tête.
Ris Yette, ris, Yette de **Tours**

(b) *Malheureuse Adèle.*

1

Ni la puissance des monarques
Le jeunesse ni la beauté
Rien n'est donc à l'abri des Parques,
Tout doit subir leur cruauté!
Malheureuse Adèle,
Hier jeune et belle,
De ses chansons elle charmait les bois:
Et plus jamais sa chère voix
N'appellera ses compagnes fidèles.
Adèle? Elle est morte, Adèle!

2

En vain le ciel de l'Italie
Plus d'un célèbre praticien
Défendirent sa chère vie:
Contre le sort nul ne peut rien.
Préparez pour elle
La pâle asphodèle
De tous cotés les funèbres échos
Répèteront ces tristes mots
Dont gémiront les blanches tourterelles:
Adèle? Elle est morte, Adèle!

"Rillettes" and "Mortadelle" are always served as hors-d'œuvre. The former is a great delicacy from Angers, Saumur and Tours. The latter is of Italian origin.

that, since he had to play Siegfried's fanfare out of sight in the wings during performances, this was the first time he had ever been clapped.

The last diners to leave would be those from the boxes, into which they could steal without disturbing anyone as the lights were lowered – and also, if she was present, Nellie Melba who, according to Boulestin 'always treated German music in the Italian fashion'. After the performance the star singers themselves would sup at the restaurant.

There came a period, following the Wall Street crash, when the depression affected business and Boulestin had a bright idea for attracting musical gourmets. He prepared a menu in which each dish was accompanied by appropriate melodies, and engaged Mme Sophie Wyss to sing Schubert's 'The Trout', Poulenc's 'The Carp', Ravel's 'Guinea Fowl', Chabrier's 'Ducklings', Auric's 'Black Hen' and 'Little Apple', with H. Villa Lobos's 'The Market' as an *apéritif-prèlude*. The printed programme for this *Petit Concert Gastronomique* contained Boulestin's notes which parodied those of a concert programme, and included recipes on the subjects which had inspired the composers. The concert ended with the 'Chansons à la Charcutière' by Claude Terrasse, sung by Alice Delysia.

The press gave wide publicity to the event and *The Tatler* filled two pages with photographs of the diners who included Dame Edith and Sir Osbert Sitwell, Lady Diana Cooper, Charles B. Cochran and his wife, Gladys Cooper, among the other prominent socialites. In 1981 when Michael Parkin published his *Salute to Marcel Boulestin* he made an unsuccessful attempt to persuade the new owners of the famous restaurant to hold another such concert there.

Food of all kinds occurs as a theme in so much music that it would, in fact, be easy to launch a whole series of Gastronomic Concerts. There is the ninth number of the orchestral suite originally composed by Richard Strauss as a curtain-raiser for the Stuttgart première of his opera, *Ariadne auf Naxos*, entitled 'The Dinner-Table Music and Dance of the Young Kitchen Servants', which suggests with its sounds the various courses (music reminiscent of Wagner's *Das Rheingold* is heard when the waiter serves the Rhine salmon, for example).

We have also Haydn's 'Trout Quintet', the first to be written for piano and strings; the Fisherman's Chorus from Auber's *La Muette de Portici*; Ponchielli's 'Pescator, affonda l'esca'; various anglers' songs and folksongs like 'The Crabfish'. These could be followed by L. Compton's 'My grandfather had some very fine ducks'; J. P. F. Hartmann's 'Fly, birdie, fly'; the Kentucky mountain ditty, 'The Barnyard Song', and the old English folksong, 'Adam the Poacher'; followed by Moussorgsky's 'Gathering mushrooms'; the folksong 'Gathering peascods'; and (for fun with the lettuce) the Russian 'Caterpillar! Caterpillar!' To finish – 'Cherry ripe', or 'Cherries and plums'. The meal could be accompanied with Scottish airs like 'O, whar gat ye that hauver-meal bannock'; and 'Drink to me only with thine eyes' or 'Gae bring to me a pint o' wine'. To admonish those who aren't eating, or who won't order unusual dishes, perhaps Schumann's 'Why are you ill and drooping?' And finishing, possibly, with hymns of praise to the chef.

It might add to the joys of cooking if a stove were invented emulating the Count de Castil Maria's marvellous turnspit. As it rotated the meat and game before the kitchen fire in his home at Treviso, it played twenty-four different tunes on an organ. 'The Roast Beef of Old England' indicated that a sirloin was ready for the table, while other airs warned the chef to remove the fowl *à la Flamande* or the leg of lamb *à l'Anglaise*.

Music itself, of course, can conjure up different images, depending on one's temperament. A nineteenth-century critic wrote that the compositions of Berlioz made him think of 'a dish of yesterday's whitebait, all heads and tails and fragments, and very little body'. To admirers, on the other hand, such music played while they were eating poor food, wretchedly cooked, might render them oblivious of its defects and maybe even help them enjoy it. So try the effects of appropriate records on your guests. Like a superb sauce, Callas may cast her charm over the croquettes or Pavarotti perk up the pot-luck.

★
The Café Momus
★

If asked whether the Café Momus were a real or an imaginary place, it is probable that some opera-goers might give the wrong answer, especially since it no longer exists outside productions of *La Bohème*. Once situated in the rue des Prêtres-Saint-Germain-l'Auxerrois, the Café (where Act II of Puccini's opera is set) first became famous through Henri Murger's book, *Scènes de la vie de Bohème*. The 'First Bohemian', as Murger has been called, was the son of the concierge of an apartment house, 5 rue des Trois-Frères, where he spent his childhood and youth and where also lived Luigi Lablache, the great international bass. This giant, with an appetite to match and a most engaging personality, became Queen Victoria's singing teacher. 'An organ more richly toned or suave than his voice was never given to mortal,' wrote the eminent critic, H. F. Chorley. 'A grander head was never more grandly set on human shoulders . . . His shoe was as big as a child's boat. One could have clad the child in one of his gloves.' Musical gourmets might indeed be proud to have this Brobdingnagian in their ranks. Also in that apartment house lived Manuel Garcia the elder, a superb Spanish tenor who was a brilliant *maestro di canto*, and whose daughters were to rise to fame as the divas Maria Malibran and Pauline Viardot.

Henri Murger became a habitué of the Café Momus where a cup of coffee cost only 5 sous. He wrote later in his book:

> Gustave Colline the great philosopher, Marcel the great painter, Schaunard the great musician, and Rodolphe the great poet, as they liked to call one another, were regular patrons of the Café Momus. They were known as the Four Musketeers because they were inseparable, and sometimes did not pay what they owed . . . They met in a room large enough to accommodate forty customers, but where no one else cared to stay on account of their behaviour. A first-time visitor to the Café who innocently entered their

lair would soon hurry out leaving his coffee hardly touched
and his paper unread – for the opinions expressed on art
and the topics of the day turned the cream sour. Indeed,
the waiter who used to serve the four friends thought they
must be mad.

The Café's smoking-room was actually frequented by many
more than four writers and artists, and they were all Bohemians
who, contemptuous of bourgeois niceties, devised a scheme for
buying only one cup of coffee. When it was, say, X's turn to be
the first to arrive, he would order a cup and take it up to their
den. Then Y would rush in asking whether X was there, and on
being told he was, would bound upstairs shouting: 'Must see
him urgently!' The others followed, employing similar tactics;
so for an outlay of only 5 sous they all had the use of the
smoking-room where they would lounge in comfortable
armchairs, read the newspapers freely provided, play back-
gammon, thump the piano, and order glasses of water.

It was fortunate for these Bohemians that Louvet, owner of
the Café Momus, was a failed author who felt sorry for those
whom, like himself, fate had neglected. Nevertheless, accept-
ing a nightly income of 5 sous for a solitary cup of coffee in
return for the use of a room that could accommodate up to forty
paying customers was a recipe for financial ruin. It was surprising that Louvet managed to survive for four years. Then in
1848, when almost bankrupt, he announced that he had discovered, buried away in an attic, two trunks packed with
manuscripts by Jean-Baptiste Louvet de Couvray, author of the
erotic eighteenth-century novel, *Les Amours du Chevalier de
Faubles*. When this became generally known, a horde of
journalists, bibliomaniacs, bibliopoles, and the sex-crazy
besieged the Café, to be told by Louvet that he had already sold
the manuscripts and had sworn not to reveal the name of the
purchaser. But the publicity attracted so many moneyed people
that business boomed, and many became regular customers. As
a result, Louvet became prosperous enough to take over the
Café de la Rotonde at the Palais-Royal, which he completely

redecorated and refurnished with such elegance that no true Bohemian would deign to enter it.

Henri Murger, meanwhile, had also deserted the Bohemians, and in February 1845 he began contributing humorous anecdotes about them to *Le Corsaire*. These proved popular, and encouraged him to write a short story, *Un Envoyé de la Providence*, about a young painter, Marcel, who lacks a black coat without which he cannot accept an invitation to attend a society dinner. A wealthy bourgeois suddenly arrives and asks to have his portrait painted. He is persuaded to take off his black coat and wear a smoking jacket instead, on the pretext that it will make him look more distinguished on canvas. Schaunard, Marcel's friend, then keeps the sitter entertained until the painter returns from his dinner. In March 1846 a second tale by Murger was published, telling of the love of a poet, Rodolphe, for Louise, a working-class girl. Four months later, in Murger's next piece, Mimi first appears. These and the following stories were autobiographical, based on Murger's own love affairs. Payment for them was poor, only 15 francs for each contribution, and he lived such a precarious existence that twice in 1848, weak from months of near-starvation, he begged the editor of *Le Corsaire* to let him have money to buy food. The second time he wrote from hospital, promising in return to send him copy in instalments twice a week. Murger's last story was published in April 1849.

Théodore Barrière, a young clerk in the Ministry of War who had had sketches performed on the professional stage, suddenly called on the First Bohemian in his leaky garret and suggested basing a play on his stories. They collaborated, and Barrière submitted the script to Thibaudeau who ran the Théâtre des Variétés. He liked what he read but said it would be impossible to dress the cast as the costumiers had no Hungarian clothes in stock; Barrière explained that the characters were not gypsies from Bohemia but simply unconventional Parisians, and Thibaudeau became more interested, finally making up his mind on realizing how little the sets would cost him. The ones he used were so tatty that the authors complained, but were curtly told:

'Don't interfere, gentlemen. I was living that sort of life long before you invented Bohemia.'

The première was a triumph and the critics were unanimous in their praise. Théophile Gautier wrote: 'Nobody has ever witnessed such pyrotechnics of wit . . . But M. Murger's wit is full of emotion: laughter with him is close to tears and has none of that heartless brilliance that hurts . . . One can tell that this work was lived before it was written.'

On the evening before the first night, Michel Levy, an astute publisher, invited Murger and Barrière to be his guests at the celebrated Maison D'Or, and over supper offered Murger an immediate payment of 500 francs in gold for the rights to publish all his stories in book form. The First Bohemian agreed on the spot. Within a week, he had abandoned his seedy attic and was living among the hitherto despised bourgeoisie. He informed a friend: 'I have a splendid roof over my head. I have rented a luxurious flat with my own front door, which has every possible modern comfort.'

In 1851 *Scènes de la vie de Bohème* was published, and in a preface Murger made it quite clear that he had indeed joined the enemy. 'Bohemia is the probationary period in an artist's life; it is the waiting-room to the Academy, the Hôtel-Dieu or the Morgue.' Bohemians, he said, could be divided into classes, the largest of which were those 'impoverished artists condemned to life-long obscurity because they cannot or will not find a means of publicizing their artistic existence and of proving, by what they already are, what they might one day become.' And so their days were spent 'on the fringe of society in isolation and inertia'. Fortune did not even know their addresses and they waited in vain 'for pedestals to come and place themselves under their feet'.

Murger also castigated 'the amateur Bohemians' – well-to-do young men who enjoyed moving in a rebellious set, 'for whom going without dinners every day, sleeping out in the open as uncomfortably as possible, and wearing nankeen suits in December represents the peak of human happiness'. Becoming bored with posing as Bohemians, these amateurs eventually drifted back to their small-town homes, married, and became solicitors and the like. Then 'sitting by the fire on a winter's evening, they boast of their poverty-stricken lives as artists with the exaggeration of travellers describing a tiger-hunt'.

Scènes de la vie de Bohème contained an ironic epilogue, set a year after Mimi's death. Musette has married and Marcel is now a fashionable portrait-painter. On meeting Rodolphe again, he asks, 'Where are you eating this evening?' The other answers, 'If you like, we might go and have a twelve-sous dinner in that old haunt of ours in the rue du Four where the plates are of rough pottery and where we were still ravenous when we had finished the meal.' 'No, thank you!' Marcel cries. 'I don't mind talking about the past, but only over a bottle of vintage wine, and seated in a well-upholstered chair in an elegant restaurant. What do you expect? I've been corrupted. Now I like only the best.'

More than forty years later, in March 1893 when Murger's book was no longer in copyright, Leoncavallo and Puccini chanced to meet in a Milan café. Each had won acclaim during the previous year; the former for *I Pagliacci* and the latter for *Manon Lescaut*. As they chatted, it seems that Puccini remarked that he was composing the score for a new opera based on Murger's book. The news infuriated Leoncavallo, who declared that he was engaged on an identical project and reminded the other that before starting to compose he had offered the libretto to Puccini, who had turned it down.

The dispute excited the operatic world when reported in the newspapers. Puccini's opera was the first to be staged: Toscanini conducted the première at the Teatro Regio of Turin on 1 February 1896. Although the audience received it well, the notices were mainly adverse. The most influential critic, Carlo Borsezio, pontificated: '*La Bohème* will leave only a slight trace in the history of our opera.' One solitary reviewer from Genoa correctly foresaw 'a triumphal future for this work'.

Leoncavallo's *La Bohème* was not completed until fifteen months later, and, thanks largely to the young Caruso's brilliant début as Rodolfo, it had a rapturous reception when first presented in Venice. However, although early indications suggested that it might eclipse Puccini's opera, the final arbiter in these matters – public taste – decided otherwise.

 Composers at the table

★
Rossini, the genial gastronome
★

Music, says Shakespeare, is the food of love – but some musicians' love is food, and 'Food, Glorious Food', Lionel Bart's famous song from *Oliver*, might well be among the discs they would select to have with them on a desert island. Handel's girth, for instance, was gargantuan. Once he booked a table for three at a tavern, choosing dishes for that number in advance. At the time arranged he sat down, and, after five minutes had passed, impatiently demanded to know why the soup had not been served. The waiter replied that he was waiting for the company to arrive. 'Den pring up de tinner prestissimo,' growled the composer. 'I am de gompany.'

Another gormandizer was the pianist Jan Ladislav Dussek, who frequented the Ship Tavern at Greenwich in the late 1790s and who would feast in the long room overlooking the Thames on a large dish of boiled eels, one of fried flounders, another of veal cutlets, a boiled fowl, and a couple of tarts. He died from over-eating.

Jean-Baptiste Lully, King Louis XIV's chief musician, spent his spare time in the kitchen inventing recipes for stews; Bellini doted on spaghetti; and the culinary brilliance of that prince of violinists, Paganini, took second place only to his fiddling. Edward Grieg was also a great epicure. Looking at a superb display of culinary art in a restaurant window, he said to the American composer, Frank Van Der Stucken, 'What an ideal symphony! How perfect in all its details, in form, content, and instrumentation!'

More cordon-bleu recipes have been named after Rossini than any other composer – the most prized of all honours for a gourmet such as he was. He once wrote: 'The stomach is the conductor who rules the grand orchestra of our passions. An empty stomach is to me like a bassoon which growls with discontent or a piccolo flute which expresses its desire in shrill tones. A full stomach, on the other hand, is the triangle of

Gioacchino Rossini: a caricature. More cordon-bleu recipes were named after him than after any other composer

pleasure, or the drum of joy. To eat, to love, to sing, to digest –
these are, in truth, the four acts of the comic opera we call life.
Who ever let it pass without having enjoyed them is a consum-
mate ass.'

When the owner of Rossini's favourite provisions store asked
him for an autographed photograph, the composer gave him
one signed: '*To my stomach's best friend.*' He would astonish
people by maintaining that he had taken up the wrong profes-
sion and that his artistry in dressing a salad pleased him more
than all his successes in music. He once wrote to a friend:
'What is going to interest you much more than my opera is
the discovery I have just made of a new salad [dressing] for
which I hasten to send you the recipe. Take Provence oil,
French vinegar, a little lemon juice, pepper and salt. Whisk
and mix all together. Then throw in a few truffles, which you
have taken care to cut into tiny pieces. The truffles give to this
seasoning a kind of nimbus to plunge the gourmet into an
ecstasy.'

At home, Rossini enjoyed himself most when he was cooking
in the kitchen. He was extremely fond of pasta and in particular
of *cappelletti in brodo*, which was full of cheese, buttermilk curd,
egg, nutmeg, cloves and grated bread cooked in meat broth. He
would gulp it all down at a tremendous rate, as if he feared
someone might steal it from him. As a result of the ill-effects on
his health of such gorging he was continually resorting to cures
of various kinds.

When asked why he had not become a chef, Rossini replied,
'Because my education as a boy was so bad.' The aroma of his
favourite foods helped him to compose. The day before his
opera, *Tancredi*, had its première in Venice, Mme Malanotte
who was to play the title role found fault with her first aria.
Rossini went home wondering what he could compose in its
stead to please her. He told his servant to fry some rice and as he
supervised its cooking he had an inspiration and noted down the
beautiful melody, 'Di tanti palpiti', afterwards known as the
aria di rizzi – the rice aria.

In Paris, the composer lived in a most suitable location for such a gourmet – near the Boulevard des Italiens, above the Café Foy known as Chez Bignon's after its affable owner. In a letter from Paris dated 3 January 1865, to Sir Michael Costa the conductor, who had sent him some Stilton cheese as a Christmas present, Rossini wrote: 'Today, invigorated by that delicious cheese and full of its taste, I offer you great gratitude from my stomach and from my heart! Now more than ever, I am certain that by often indulging in Stilton cheese (which I feel you do) one is able to compose fine works, and gallops in prosperity with one's head crowned with laurels.'

On 28 May 1866, Rossini thanks his 'beloved' Costa for some Cheddar: 'The cheese sent to me is worthy of a Bach, of a Handel, of a Cimarosa, indeed of an old Pesarese like myself! I did not hurry to acknowledge it because I wished to know to the full the worth of your generous gift. For three consecutive days I ate of it, moistening it with the best wines of my cellars, for instance, Xeres, Madeira, Alicante, etc. And I swear I never ate better food than your "Chedor chese" [*sic*] – may the Britannic autography be cursed.'

In view of Rossini's passion for the pleasures of the table, it is not surprising to learn that when the people of his native Pesaro decided to erect a statue of him, he wistfully remarked that it would have made him far happier had they presented him with several kilos of mortadella sausages, or a fat duck or a goose – but not a turkey, which he claimed was 'too big for one to eat and not big enough for two.'

Neither is it surprising that in composing his operas, Rossini should so have arranged matters as to make provision for his feeding habits. In some of his works, the oboist plays only at the beginning and end of the first act. This, the story goes, was because he had to prepare a snack for Rossini to eat during the first interval.

After marrying a superb cook, Rossini was greatly disappointed when, following the ceremony, she refused ever again to cook for him. He found solace in fine restaurants such as the Maison D'Or whose celebrated chef, Casimir-Moisson, was President of the first Académie de Cuisine de France. The genial gastronome was particularly fond of foie gras, which is an ingredient of most of the dishes named after him.

★
Haydn, recipe collector
★

A butcher's daughter about to be wed was very fond of Haydn's music, so the father called on the great man and asked if it were at all possible for him to compose something in celebration of the event. Kind-hearted Haydn said he would, and within twenty-four hours sent him a minuet. A few days later the composer heard the piece being played in the road below his study window, and, looking out, he was astonished to see an enormous, gaily decorated ox with gilded horns, accompanied by a band and the butcher, who said: 'I thought, sir, that the most appropriate way in which I could show my appreciation was by offering you the finest ox I own.' Haydn at first tried to refuse the gift but eventually accepted it, not wanting to offend the grateful father, and thereafter the piece was called the 'Ox' Minuet.

(Years later, an ox, an elephant, an ape, and some horses, together with soldiers, priests, and vestal virgins, took part in Luigi Mangotti's ballet-opera, *Amor*, which Giulio Gatti-Casazza presented at La Scala, Milan. There was a lively dress rehearsal, with Papus, the elephant, charging the humans, on top of whom part of the scenery collapsed. The première, nevertheless, went well and audiences filled the opera-house until one night the ape snapped its chain and, running amok, caused such a panic among the spectators that the police had to be called and all further performances were cancelled. Shortly after this, a large notice appeared in the window of a nearby butcher: '*Meat of the famous ox of the ballet* Amor *sold here.*')

In late 1789, Haydn spent some time in Vienna where he

received much hospitality from Marianne de Genzenger, wife of a gynaecologist who often entertained the musical celebrities of the capital in her home at Scottenhof. On returning to the seclusion of Esterház, Haydn wrote to her:

The good Viennese pastries are already a thing of the past. Ah, yes, I say to myself, thinking of all this in my own house, having to eat a piece of quinquagenarian beef instead of delicious roast veal, a piece of yellowing mutton instead of a *ragoût aux croquettes*, a slice of roast leather instead of *faisan à la Bohémienne*, one of those stews called *Gross-Salat* instead of those excellent and delicately flavoured oranges, one of those dried apple puffs instead of those heavenly *pâtisseries*; ah, yes, I say to myself if only now I had a store of those pâtés which I could not eat in Vienna! Here at Esterház no one asks me, 'Would you like some chocolate? With or without milk? Or coffee, perhaps? Would you like an ice-cream? Vanilla or pineapple?' If only I had a good piece of Parmesan, especially during Lent, I would put it on my vermicelli. I have just asked our concierge to send me some pounds of it.

Forgive me, most gracious of women, for wasting your time with such trifles and such a miserable scribble. Forgive a man to whom the Viennese have shown so much kindness. I must get used to the country, little by little. Yesterday I worked for the first time . . .

Haydn did not remain long in solitary Esterház. Within a few weeks he was off to England. That he had a keen interest in all to do with food is apparent from the account of his visit in note-books where he jotted down recipes gathered from a variety of sources. A sea-captain told him how to make 'noyen' – a drink from Martinique prepared from nutmeg, rum and sugar. He also learned how to preserve cream or milk for a long time: 'One takes a bottle full of milk and puts it in an earthen-ware pot or copper vessel containing water enough to cover more than half of the bottle, and then places it over a fire and seals it securely, so that no air can escape, and in this way the milk will keep for many months. NB: the bottle must be firmly corked before it is placed in the water.'

When Haydn returned to England the following spring, the *Public Advertiser* for 12 April 1792 reported: 'Haydn finds the good cheer of this country in such concert *pitch* with his own *great taste* that he has declared his intention of concluding the *finale* of his days with the *Roast Beef of Old England*.'

The next year, Haydn came back to London. He had become very friendly with George, Prince of Wales, and on 23 June 1793 he set down in that treasured notebook the First Gentleman in Europe's much-esteemed recipe for punch made from one bottle each of champagne, burgundy, and rum, with 10 lemons, 2 oranges, and 1½ lbs of sugar.

Haydn enjoyed travelling, for it took him away from his shrewish wife, Anna Maria Keller, who tormented him by using his manuscripts as curlpapers for her hair and as pastry-tin liners. She must at least have been grateful for the meat provided by that ox. When Max Réger played the piano in a performance of Schubert's 'Trout' Quintet he was delighted to receive afterwards from admirers a basketful of trout, so he announced that at his next recital the programme would include Haydn's 'Ox' Minuet. But no one took the hint.

★
Auber, the hedonist

★

Daniel Auber's *Masaniello* was Queen Alexandra's favourite opera. The elegant director of the Paris Conservatoire was happiest surrounded by attractive women and lived in a tastefully furnished house where he gave splendid dinner-parties at which he never allowed music to be discussed. Most of his operas had their premières at the Opéra-Comique, and if the prima donna in it were beautiful (which he saw to it she invariably was), Auber would rehearse her on his own, in private. On one such occasion the composer proved what a musician he was by playing the accompaniment on the piano with his left hand while the experienced fingers of his right hand discovered all the soprano's concealed charms. So well-trained an artist was she that her roulades went on soaring forth without a tremor.

As Auber preferred to eat at home or in private, it is perhaps not surprising that only one of his operas inspired a restaurant's chef, and that was *Fra Diavolo*.

★

Berlioz and the free supper
★

In his *Evenings in the Orchestra*, Hector Berlioz relates how Liszt and Rubini once found only about fifty people in the audience for their first recital in a certain town. Rubini was so disgusted that he told Liszt, 'I refuse to sing.' 'I disagree,' replied the great pianist. 'On the contrary, you must sing at your very best. Our audience is clearly composed of the élite among music-lovers in this part of the country, and you must treat them as such. Let us do justice to ourselves.' And to set Rubini an example, he played the first piece superbly. Then the tenor sang, in his most disdainful *voix mixte*.

After Liszt had ended his third number with such impressive execution that the tiny audience rewarded him with delighted applause, he went to the front of the platform and asked them if they would like to give him the pleasure of having them as his guests at supper. There was but a moment's hesitation, then, realizing the uniqueness of such an opportunity, all vociferously accepted the invitation. The meal cost Liszt 1,200 francs. The two artists then cancelled their remaining concerts and left the town. Berlioz, telling the story, comments that this was surely a mistake, for there would almost certainly have been standing-room only at the next recital, in expectation of a free supper.

Commenting further on the power of food to attract people, Berlioz describes how one day he met a prominent pianist-composer who had returned from a seaport where he had hoped to give a recital. 'I saw no possibility of giving a concert there,' he told Berlioz, 'so I abandoned the idea. You see, the herring catch had just been unloaded and the whole town was thinking of nothing but this precious treasure.' Berlioz sympathized with him, saying, 'How, indeed, is a man to fight against a shoal of fish?'

★
Massenet

★

A number of dishes were named after Massenet and his operas, *Manon* and *Thaïs*, by chefs of restaurants in Paris. He himself was more of a ladies' man than a gourmet. Léon Daudet, in his *Fantômes et vivants*, described entertainingly but with a certain satirical exaggeration the composer's visits to the Daudet home. On arrival, he said, Massenet never failed to go round the salon paying fulsome compliments, finding even the plainest beautiful and praising the artistic and literary work of those present. 'After this, he would settle himself in an armchair and behave as if he were a child or a pet which must be fed. Milk and cake would be brought to him, and as he drank thirstily and scattered crumbs, he indulged in small talk . . . The old ladies, who never tired of telling him how much they adored music, he would treat as though they were pretty nestlings. Then his roving eye would notice some truly young and beautiful woman demurely remaining at a distance from him. Immediately he would make towards her, fall upon his hands and knees, perform a kind of Pyrrhic dance or any clowning he considered might amuse or tease his quarry. This pantomime was accompanied by lovesick looks begging swift surrender. He had all the easily excited exhibitionism of the lyre-bird or the peacock. But the restrictive rules of bourgeois society still operated, husbands might be around . . . so Massenet would be forced to curb his ardour. Moving to the piano, he would then become a changed being, in whom one recognized greatness.'

Massenet's *Manon* was rapturously received at its Opéra-Comique première in January 1884, and though the critics were lukewarm its popular appeal proved so tremendous that after running in that theatre's repertoire for ten years, it had made some 2,000,000 francs for the box office. By 1970 it had been presented more than 2,000 times there alone, and was second only in popularity to *Carmen*.

A husband once confided in Massenet that his wife no longer loved him, so the composer gave him two tickets for *Manon*, telling him to take her to hear it, and each time she cried to caress her hand. The man agreed to try the experiment. A few days later Massenet met him, and seeing that he looked more miserable than ever, asked, 'Didn't it work? Didn't you clasp your wife's hand at the sentimental moments?' The other nodded gloomily and said, 'But when I tried to seize her hand during the third act, I found that both of them were already tightly held by the fellow on the other side of her.' 'My friend,' the composer commented, 'that proves he was more of a musician than you.'

Thaïs, based on Anatole France's novel, had its first night at the Paris *Opéra* on 16 March 1894, with violet-eyed Sybil Sanderson in the title role. At one tense moment, a hook came loose on her ravishing costume and it parted like stage curtains in front, showing her completely naked to the waist. Reviewing the performance, the critic Willy (husband of Colette) made a punning reference to Sybil as 'Seinderson', and went on, 'She appeared much put out by the mishap, and not to know to which breast to turn to next.'

★
No bear's paws for Offenbach
★

Jacques Offenbach, celebrated for his can-can music, was probably the lightest and shortest of well-known composers, never weighing more than fifty kilos or measuring more than five feet in height. His appetite was poor, and his lunch in Paris usually consisted of a boiled egg, a tender noisette of lamb, a spoonful or two of potato, asparagus in season, a little fruit (in summer, two or three strawberries), followed by what he liked best – a Havana cigar. This was all he ordered at the chic restaurants he frequented, where a table was always kept ready in case he arrived and a swarm of sycophants buzzed round him. For business deals he reserved a private room which he termed a *'cabineto particolioso'*.

Offenbach's custom was divided between the Café Riche next door to him, the Maison D'Or, Chez Bignon's, and Peters. He ceased visiting the latter when its owner acquired a performing bear which nearly scratched him when he offered it a lump of sugar. Shortly after this, the animal attacked a waiter and had to be killed. Peters then invited back his distinguished client to be served with a scarce dish – bear's paws. Offenbach came, toyed with the meat, pushed it aside, and lit a cigar . . . but he did resume his patronage of the restaurant.

When the 'Mozart of the Champs-Elysées' (as admirers called Offenbach) had to attend rehearsals in the early afternoon, he would have his frugal lunch sent up to his apartment from the Café Riche. His daughters quarrelled among themselves for the privilege of serving him, because they knew he would leave most of the food and the fortunate girl could then eat it herself. On one occasion he told his family he longed for peaches, which were then scarce; after searching Paris, the daughters managed to buy some at the exorbitant price of 20 francs each. As they expected, their father had already lost interest in the fruit and did not even put one on his plate, so the happy girls disposed of them.

Jacques Offenbach: a poor appetite and no taste for bears'
paws

After visiting the United States, Offenbach wrote entertainingly of his experiences there, declaring that if he had eaten
and drunk all that was offered him he would never have
returned alive to France. 'They stuff their guests in America
like the Breton women do the breasts of their fat turkeys. I
became better known as a composer through staying in New
York, but, alas, I made my wretched gout worse.' In New
York, he said, he found everything except a person who knew

more than one language: among the 200 waiters in the Fifth Avenue Hotel, nobody spoke French. On entering its immense dining-room, Offenbach was met by a tall *maître d'hôtel* who, instead of asking him where he would like to sit, pointed peremptorily at a table. This autocrat sat diners next to whomever he pleased, and ignored what they said. The first thing the waiter did was to bring Offenbach a glass of iced water that he did not want: looking round, the composer says he noticed that at not one of the fifty tables in the room was anything being drunk but iced water. 'If ever you should find wine or beer before a diner, you can be certain he is a European.' Next, Offenbach was handed a menu listing no less than eighty *plats du jour*, and discovered that he was expected to choose at least three or four, which to his amazement were all served at the same time. 'If you forget to order a vegetable, you will be brought every one of the fifteen vegetables on the menu, with the result that you find yourself suddenly surrounded by some thirty plates of soup, fish, meat, jam, etc., including ten varieties of dessert. All drawn up in battle array defy your stomach. The first time it makes you dizzy and destroys your appetite.' As a result, unable to endure this after a few days, the composer went to live in a private house.

Out of curiosity, Offenbach nevertheless dined at fashionable restaurants both in New York and Philadelphia. He came to the conclusion that, though Americans ran them, the actual cuisine was always French, Italian, Spanish, or German, and that nothing was more difficult for a foreigner than 'to eat an American meal in that country'.

The restaurants that fascinated him most were those where food was free, provided that one bought something to drink even if it cost only ten cents. Sundays were the best days to eat there because, owing to police regulations, no alcoholic beverage could be sold – but lunch was still served *gratis*. Offenbach stressed that all the dishes were first class. At Brunswick's he noted what was available on the free menu: a delicious ham, a huge joint of roast beef, bacon and beans, potato salad, olives, pickles, cheese and biscuits. The *pièce de résistance* was the beef, and customers could cut themselves as many slices as they wished. Next to the counter where this fine fare was available were knives, forks, and spoons, but most of the men preferred to use their fingers. 'Some even plunged their hands into the salad bowl as they helped themselves. I am still shuddering over that. When I told the head waiter how horribly unhygienic I considered this behaviour, he made excuses, saying, "It shocks us less than it does you. Time is money to these gentlemen, and they are in a hurry."'

The service was lethargically casual, and one might be left with that iced water for ages before receiving any further attention. A different waiter was in charge of the menu and would not part with it. Yet another kept the wine list, whilst uncorking the bottle one ordered was the prerogative of a fourth mournful waiter – or at least it was thus at the Hotel Brunswick. After this exasperating ritual had been repeated a number of times, the composer rebelled and told the *maître d'hôtel* that if he were treated in such a manner again, that would be the last time they saw him in the restaurant. The next day, when Offenbach arrived for lunch, all the twenty or thirty waiters were lined up awaiting him, each one respectfully holding a corkscrew in his hand. Since that day, Offenbach wrote, 'You don't have to wait at Brunswick's.'

The evening following his arrival in New York, Offenbach entertained some American friends to dinner in his suite at the Fifth Avenue Hotel. After the soup had been served, he was amazed to hear the waiter whistling. Timid at first, the man became increasingly bold, and according to Offenbach, 'Soon he was attempting little trills, and gradually he attacked the grandest melodies. Sometimes the tunes were sad, then suddenly for no apparent reason they became lively and cheerful.' At the end of the meal, the composer reproved the waiter for whistling. 'Oh, sir, I'm sorry,' he replied. 'You see I'm a music-lover and I use it to express my feelings. When I don't like a dish, I whistle sad tunes. When a dish pleases me, I whistle something jolly. And when I really dote on what I'm serving, I . . .'

'Like the *bombe glacée*?' Offenbach interrupted.

'So you noticed that, sir? Then I whistle my gayest tunes.'

'You find that tune from the *Grand Duchess* – the one you were whistling – gay?'

'I do, sir. It's a gentleman's tune, so amusing.'

All his life Offenbach detested whistling, and in Paris he had sacked a valet for doing so. He writes: 'As I do not like people whistling my music, I asked the *maître d'hôtel* never again to have me served by that whistling waiter.'

Offenbach had trouble with another waiter when dining at Pétry's in Philadelphia with a friend. They ordered a julienne, and the waiter grimaced. 'I don't recommend that. The vegetables they use up – how can they do it?'

'All right, we'll do without soup. You have salmon?'

'Certainly we have it. We've had it for a very long time. It's not what you would call fresh.'

'Then a rare beefsteak.'

'The cook ruins them.'

'Strawberries.'

'Mushy and tasteless.'

'Cheese?'

'I'll ask it to come up. Won't need any help. It can walk alone.'

Offenbach says he reprimanded the man for being so disloyal to his employer, and added, 'If I were Pétry, I should fire you.'

The fellow retorted, 'He hasn't waited for your advice. This is my last night here,' gave a low bow, and left.

Despite such talk, ends the composer, they had an admirable dinner.

Before returning to France, Offenbach was entertained to supper at Delmonico's by a theatrical director who had invited the stars of his company to join them. After the meal was finished, they remained in the private room, smoking and drinking. The composer noticed to his surprise that one of the waiters kept returning and listening to their conversation. Not being the host, Offenbach made no comment, especially as nobody else in the party appeared to find the man's conduct objectionable. As there were still a few days left before Offen-bach sailed, he invited the director and the artists to have supper with him at the same restaurant, and once again, following the serving of coffee, a waiter came back at frequent intervals and walked silently round the table peering at each person in turn. At last Offenbach could stand this no longer and told him, 'Waiter, you have come in several times without being called. Don't let it happen again.'

'Sorry, sir,' the culprit replied, 'but Mr Delmonico has ordered us to inspect each private dining-room every five minutes.'

'Does he belong to the police that he should send you to eavesdrop on his clients?'

'I have no idea, sir. But I do know that Mr Delmonico would dismiss me if I did not carry out his instructions.'

'Does he think we are going to steal his linen and silver, or that we are capable of overlooking for a moment the fact that clients and their guests are expected to behave strictly like ladies and gentlemen in his celebrated establishment? Well, I warn you now, well in advance. It is half-past one in the morning, and we are going to remain here until seven. If you insist on obeying your employer, you will have to return sixty-six times.'

'I shall have to do that, sir.'

Offenbach writes that having made his protest, he saw no reason to punish himself by losing too much of his sleep, so they left at two o'clock declaring that Delmonico's would not see them again.

Verdi and the man pursued by spectres

While the stars of musical comedy enjoy having their arrival in a restaurant greeted by the orchestra striking up tunes from the shows in which they have made their names, some composers are irritated by this. Wilhelm Ganz relates how a friend of his called on Verdi at Montcalieri and found him in a room which he described as his dining-room, drawing-room, and bedroom combined, adding, 'I have two other large rooms, but they are full of things that I have hired for the season.' He threw open the doors and showed the visitor a collection of several dozen piano-organs. 'When I arrived here,' Verdi explained, 'all these organs played airs from *Rigoletto, Trovatore,* and my other operas from morning till night. I was so annoyed that I hired the whole lot for the season. It has cost me a 1,000 francs, but at all events I am left in peace.'

On Christmas Eve, 1871, Verdi's *Aida,* commissioned by the Khedive for the Suez Canal's gala opening, had its triumphant première at the Opera House of Cairo, followed some six weeks later by an equally well-received production at La Scala. Not everyone approved, however, for in May the composer received a letter dated the 7th of that month, from a Signor Bertani of Reggio, who wrote:

On the 2nd, attracted by the sensation which your opera, *Aida,* was making, I went to Parma. Half an hour before the performance began, I was already in my seat, No. 120. I admired the scenery, listened with great pleasure to the excellent singers and took pains to let nothing escape me. After the performance was over, I asked myself whether I was satisfied. The answer was in the negative. I returned to Reggio and on the way back in the railway compartment, I listened to the verdict of my fellow travellers. Nearly all of them agreed that *Aida* was a work of the highest rank.

So I decided to hear it again, and on the 4th went back to Parma. I made the most desperate efforts to obtain a reserved seat, and there was such a crowd that I had to spend five lire to see the performance in comfort. Afterwards I reached the conclusion that your opera contains nothing exciting or memorable, and that had it not been for the magnificent scenery the audience would not have sat through it till the end. It will fill the theatre à few more times, then gather dust in the archives.

Now, my dear Signor Verdi, you can imagine my regret at having spent 32 lire for those two performances. Add to this the aggravating circumstance that I am dependent on my family, and you will understand that this money preys on my mind like a terrible spectre. I am therefore putting the facts frankly and openly before you, so that you may reimburse me. Here are the details:

Single railway fare	2.30 lire
Return journey	3.60 lire
Theatre	8.00 lire
Disgustingly bad dinner at the station	2.00 lire
	15.90 lire
Multiplied by 2 –	31.80 lire

In the hope that you will extricate me from this dilemma,
I am, yours sincerely,
Prospero Bertani.

This letter had been sent to Verdi, care of Giulio Ricordi, who dealt with his business affairs, and the composer now sent him the following instructions.

As you may readily imagine, in order to save this scion from the spectre that pursues him, I shall gladly pay the little bill he sends me. Be so kind therefore, as to get one of your agents to send the sum of 27 lire 80 centesimi to this Signor Prospero Bertani, Via San Domenico, No. 5. True that is not the whole sum he demands, but for me to pay for his dinner, too, would be wearing the joke a bit thin. He could easily have eaten at home. Naturally, he must send you a receipt, as well as a written declaration promising never to hear another one of my new operas so that he won't expose himself again to the dangers of being pursued

[116]

Giuseppe Verdi, by Boldoni. Verdi prided himself on
knowing more about cooking than many women

by spectres, and that he may spare me further travelling expenses!

Signor Bertani promptly complied and his undertaking was preserved by Verdi among his papers. Dated 15 May 1872, it reads:

> I, the undersigned, certify herewith that I have received the sum of 27.80 lire from Maestro Giuseppe Verdi, as reimbursement of my expenses for a trip to Parma to hear the opera, *Aida*. The Maestro felt it was fair that this sum should be restored to me, since I did not find his opera to my taste. At the same time it is agreed that I shall under-take no trip to hear any of the Maestro's new operas in the future, unless he agrees to pay all expenses whatever my opinion of his work may be.

Like Rossini, Verdi was a valued customer of the renowned Maison D'Or Restaurant in Paris and to celebrate the success of *Aida* various dishes were named after him. He also prided himself on knowing much more about cooking than many women. For example, in a letter written to Teresa Stolz from Sant' Agata on 12 August 1890, Verdi wrote that he was sending her by rail two shoulders of ham, and gave these cooking instructions:

1. Put in tepid water for about 12 hours to remove salt.
2. Put it afterwards in cold water and boil over a slow fire, so it won't blow up, for about 3½ hours, perhaps 4 for the larger one. To see if it's done, prick the shoulder with a *curedents* and, if it enters easily, the shoulder is done.
3. Let it cool in its own broth and serve. Take special care in the cooking; if it is hard, it is not good, if it is overcooked it becomes dry and difficult to chew.

———————————— ★ ————————————
Wagner, food reformer
———————————— ★ ————————————

For most of his life Wagner was a meat-eater. In about 1870, when he was fifty-seven, he met Nietzsche, aged twenty-six, who was then a vegetarian as a matter of principle. 'How can you preach a gospel of energetic and dangerous living so that only the fittest will survive,' Wagner asked the philosopher, 'and yourself feed like this?' He went on to argue that the contest of all living creatures against each other made it necessary for men to get strength through their food in order to attempt and accomplish great things. That was the only way the race of supermen would come into being. The younger man was converted, and joined the carnivores.

Ironically, in his last years Wagner changed his mind and became a vegetarian. In October 1880 the *Bayreuther Blätter* devoted all its pages to a long article by him in which he claimed that the curse of civilization was meat-eating: it was against the precepts of Christ who had been born in a vegetarian community and whose Last Supper, with its emphasis on bread and wine, had advocated vegetarianism. In the swamps around Canadian lakes, he wrote, there flourished vegetarian panthers and tigers, whose carnivorous cousins in Africa owed their bloodthirstiness to living near the arid Sahara. The majority of Russian peasants died when well over eighty, thanks to a mainly vegetarian diet. In American jails, men guilty of heinous crimes had been turned into pillars of society through a carefully balanced meatless diet. 'The degeneration of the human soul has been brought about by its departure from its natural food, that of the vegetable world.'

According to Wagner, only about one-third of mankind was addicted to 'the abominable practice of flesh-eating' but they consisted of 'the degenerate and ruling portion'. He had a plan for curing these addicts. 'If there is any basis for the assumption that animal food is indispensable in the northern climate, what is to prevent our making a rationally directed transmigration to those other countries of the globe which, in view of their luxuriant productivity – the South American peninsula, for example – are capable of maintaining the present population of every country in the world?'

Oscar Wilde thought Wagner's music the most suitable for playing in restaurants, because 'it is so loud that one can talk the whole time without other people hearing what one says'.

★

Puccini and 'gastronomic anguish'

★

Puccini was a perfectionist and demanded so much rewriting and polishing from his librettist, Luigi Illica, that he would try and lessen the strain by sending Illica presents of food. On one occasion, he wrote, 'Forgive me for the mental anguish my letters cause you. As for gastronomic anguish . . . it will come with my cooking.'

Though the composer constantly mentions food in his correspondence, he preferred simple dishes and most of all those containing beans and onions. Apart from this, he liked eating wild fowl. 'I am a mighty hunter of wild fowl, beautiful women, and good libretti,' he told a friend. As a poor student at the Conservatore in Milan, he fed during his first year mainly on thin minestrone with beans. He informed his mother in November 1880: 'I fill up with thick broth, thin broth, and thinner broth. The stomach is satisfied.' A grant of 100 lire a month from Queen Margherita accompanied his scholarship, and on receiving the first instalment he treated himself to two portions of soup, the same of pasta, half a litre of wine, a square of Gorgonzola, and a cheroot, at the Osteria Aida. Later, when he sold the world rights in his first opera, *Le Villi*, to Giulio Ricordi and received an advance of 1,000 lire, he celebrated by treating himself to roast beef with mushrooms and asparagus, vintage wines, Roquefort, and strawberries.

A caricature of Puccini done in 1898: he liked simple food
and wild fowl

At the height of his fame, Puccini patronized Paganini's and
the Savoy, where François Latry asked him to be allowed to
prepare a rich Tuscan-style dish and name it after him. Puccini
declined the honour on the grounds that it would give people a
false impression of his eating habits, and his letters, indeed,
testify to the simplicity of his tastes in this respect. For
example, on 30 April 1980 he revealed to his younger brother:
'I worked till three o'clock this morning . . . Then I had a

bunch of onions for supper.' Sometimes he would chop an onion very finely and enjoy it mixed with a can of tuna fish and its oil.

Five years later, Puccini wrote to Giulio Ricordi from the Val di Nievole:

> I am sending you a small quantity of beans and two boxes of grapes. The beans are very special ones and must be cooked in this way. Put them on the fire in cold water, which should be a moderate amount – neither too much nor too little. Boil for two hours on a slow fire, and when they are cooked there should be no more than three or four spoonfuls of water. Ergo, be careful of the quantity of water.
>
> NB. When you put them on to cook, add four or five leaves of sage, two or three heads of garlic, salt and pepper, and when they, the beans, are half cooked, add a little oil to boil with them.

Puccini was a country-lover, and corresponding with a great friend, Signor Corelli, while in Paris, he confided on 10 May 1898: 'I am panting for the fragrant woods, for the free movement of my belly in wide trousers and no waistcoat.' He was a shy man, too, yet could enjoy the limelight on occasion – for we find him mentioning in 1921: 'I had a wonderful reception last night from the public . . . including the *maître d'hôtel* at the Café de Paris. The little orchestra played *Butterfly* and I had to get up and acknowledge it.' His favourite haunt, all the same, was Lake Massaciuccoli of which he owned the hunting rights and where, no matter how wretched the weather, he would hide among the reeds in a rowboat shooting duck and the small fowl known as *folighe*.

--- ★ ---
Richard Strauss and *Beinfleisch*
--- ★ ---

When Richard Strauss was in his thirties, the restaurant of the Hotel Meissl and Schadn on Vienna's Homer Markt was internationally renowned for its boiled beef specialities, of which there were no less than twenty-four varieties from which to choose. The composer was so fond of the *Beinfleisch* that he considered composing a tone poem about its merits, but after finishing his ballet, *Schlagobers*, which extolled Viennese whipped cream, he thought that another major composition devoted to an Austrian gastronomic delight might be resented by his admirers in Germany, who, like most Germans then, were hostile to everything originating in Vienna. Not wishing to risk a fall in his considerable German royalties, he abandoned the idea. 'Too bad he did!' a Viennese music critic who admired Strauss later regretted. 'A tone-poem on *Beinfleisch* might have surpassed even the transcendental beauty of "Devil and Transfiguration".'

The secret of Meissl and Schadn's success with boiled beef lay in the fact that they owned herds of cattle that were kept inside a large sugar refinery in a village north of Vienna. There the steers were fed on molasses and sugar-beet mash, which gave their meat its extraordinary marbled texture, its taste, tenderness, and juice.

With the break-up of the Hapsburg Empire, this famous restaurant went into rapid decline and it finally expired in 1945 when American Air Force bombs half destroyed it, and then Red Army soldiers burnt what remained to the ground. Now herds of cattle are no longer reared in sugar refineries, and the boiled beef served in restaurants is often tough and dry. Such a lowering of standards would have upset a gourmet such as Richard Strauss.

When he was in London, the composer's favourite eating-place was the grill-room at the Savoy. When he dined there he would concentrate all his attention on what he ate and drank, and talk as little as possible. Only once did he upset the *maître d'hôtel* – by asking for raspberry jam with his mutton-chop. Occasionally he would consent to be a guest at one of Emerald Cunard's dinner-parties, and afterwards would play selections from his *Der Rosenkavalier*.

★

Irving Berlin

★

In his impoverished youth, Irving Berlin was employed as a waiter-cum-pianist in a shabby Bowery restaurant. Visitors would later be taken there during tours of New York, and guides would point at an ancient, ill-treated piano in a corner and allege that Berlin had composed some of his best tunes sitting at its keyboard.

Drawn to the place by a fit of nostalgia one evening when he had become famous, the composer approached the piano and started to hum 'Oh, How I Hate to Get Up in the Morning'. Just then, a coach arrived and disgorged its load of sightseers. 'This historic place is where the celebrated Irving Berlin first gave birth to his immortal melodies – on that very piano you see still standing in the corner,' the guide informed them. 'Listen – the song that Bowery bum is now playing is one of his.' He made for the piano and bent over the seated 'bum'. 'Say, you!' he scoffed. 'If Irving Berlin could hear how you're murdering one of his greatest songs, he'd turn in his grave.'

Conductors and players

★
Cooking and conducting
★

Few dishes have been named after conductors. Toscanini's attitude to food can best be exemplified by his behaviour once on returning from conducting at La Scala. As his family hurried hungrily into the dining-room after waiting all evening to sup with him, he stood in their way. 'What! You can eat after such a performance?' he upbraided them. 'Shame on you! Shame!' And after locking the dining-room door, he went off to bed.

André Prévin admits that he is 'perhaps the only guy in the world who would ruin a sandwich'. He relates how one night when working at home in San Francisco he longed for a steak, so he went out and bought one. Then, not knowing quite what to do with it, he telephoned a lady friend who recommended grilling it for nine minutes on each side. Unfortunately he was without a watch, having taken his for repair, but suddenly he recalled that the Overture to Berlioz's *Roman Carnival* lasted for near enough that length of time, so, placing the steak on the grill, he hummed that piece of music to himself. Then, turning the meat over, he timed it by Berlioz once more.

Joseph Wechsberg, in *Dining at the Pavilion*, maintained that a great restaurateur, like a great conductor, heeds both a first-rate audience and a first-rate orchestra to perform. 'To be able to cast a spell over his audience, he must have full control over his orchestra. The experienced restaurateur builds his kitchen brigade and dining-room staff just as the conductor builds the various sections of his orchestra, trying to get the best experts he can afford. Having built up his orchestra, the restaurateur's job is to get people into his restaurant and keep them there.'

★

Gâteau Gottschalk

★

No dish appears to have been named after a pianist – unless the schoolboy was correct who said that the hamburger was invented by Mark Hambourg. A large 'corporation' might be an impediment when playing, which would explain why the average pianist is not a gourmand. Louis Moreau Gottschalk, born in New Orleans in 1829, did at least have a cake made, and called after him, by the King of Spain's eldest sister. He was a child prodigy, and after his brilliant début in Paris Chopin predicted that Gottschalk would become 'the king of pianists'. It was in 1851 that he played before the Spanish Royal Family and was told by the Queen Dowager's chief physician that she found him better even than Liszt, while the Infanta sent him for dessert a cake she had baked herself. This excited the envy of the Court pianist who spitefully slammed a carriage door on Gottschalk's hand, and so injured his little finger that surgeons feared they would have to amputate it. Fortunately, after three months he not only recovered its use but found it had become much more powerful, enabling him to execute certain passages with more *éclat* than before.

Gottschalk himself was extremely kind-hearted. Once, noticing a soldier staring hungrily through the window of a res-

Arturo Toscanini: a caricature by Nerman

taurant, he insisted on giving the youth all that he fancied for dinner. In April 1862 it was the pianist's turn to be splendidly entertained, when he was performing in Milwaukee. He relates in his memoirs, written in very stilted English, that the cook of the hotel where he was staying came from Bordeaux and, having heard him play there ten years previously, was 'wild with joy' at seeing the maestro again, and 'absolutely insisted on giving me a dinner'. The *cèpes à l'huile*, the salamis and the *rognons au beurre*, served with Château Lafite and Saint-Emilion, were all 'simply incomparable'. In return Gottschalk invited this cook-proprietor and his family to the concert.

Gottschalk much preferred this French cooking by a native of

Bordeaux, where 'they know how to eat', to what he was usually offered in the smart hotels of the western seaboard. In 1865 he stayed at the Cosmopolitan Hotel, San Francisco, which had a spacious restaurant, lavishly ornamented and walled with mirrors. 'The bill of fare would make Brillat-Savarin and Carême faint for joy,' Gottschalk wrote in his reminiscences. 'Vegetables in the greatest variety, fruits of all zones, tropical and temperate, and the most artistic dishes appear in the numerous nomenclature. But I am not easily taken in by the allurements of these deceptive baits, which the hotels of the West have taught me to distrust. . . . If sometimes an inexperienced traveller falls into the snare, he either receives this answer from the waiter, "There is no more of it," and he thus preserves one illusion more; or else the phoenix asked for is served up to him, and then he swears (but a little too late) that he will never ask for it again.' However, to Gottschalk's delight, the Cosmopolitan's fare proved excellent.

It was here during this visit to California that Gottschalk had an amusing experience. Having performed the March from *Tannhäuser*, arranged by himself, on fourteen pianos, this had proved such a success that he announced a second concert. The night before it, one of his pianists was taken ill. Should Gottschalk put off the event?

'Never!' he wrote. 'The public is flighty, capricious, pitiless. Learn to seize the hour that is favourable to you – if you do not, it escapes you without any reason. Announce only thirteen pianos? Another error, still more dangerous. The public wish to hear fourteen pianos, and if you give it one less, it will think itself robbed. It demands fourteen pianos in full view on the platform. Should you place some mannikin on it [the fourteenth], the public will be satisfied . . . The proprietor of the hall, seeing my embarrassment, offered to speak to his son, an amateur pianist (he said) of the first class, who played Thalberg, Liszt, and Gottschalk without difficulty, and for whom it would be only child's play to take the part that was wanted for the March from *Tannhäuser*.'

Experience had taught Gottschalk to beware of amateurs who

play everything brilliantly at first sight, but the man spoke of his son with such assurance that he accepted the offer. However, he insisted on a rehearsal. 'At the end of two bars, I knew what I had to rely on. It was not that he played badly, if he played at all. The most complaisant ear would have hardly been able to distinguish any shreds of Wagner's theme which were floating here and there like waifs in the midst of an ocean of false notes, in a deafening storm of continuous pedal . . . My position became horrible. To refuse his assistance – the assistance of the first amateur in San Francisco, elegant and rich, who had probably caused to be circulated among all his friends and all the good society of the city [the fact] that he deigned to give me the use of his talent. It was impossible.'

The rehearsal was short. Gottschalk made no comment. The father, beaming with pride, said, 'Ah ha! What did I tell you?' His son, convinced of his own worth, smiled and kept saying how easy the piece was to play.

They parted. Gottschalk thought of feigning illness so as to cancel the concert. Then his tuner, a resourceful fellow, said, 'Sir, if this young man plays, you're going to have trouble with the other pianists. It's absolutely necessary to stop his being heard, and the only way to do it is this.' He opened the top of the upright piano intended for the amateur, took out the whole of the interior mechanism and, with a sly grin, added, 'The keyboard remains, but I assure you there will be no more false notes.'

The hall was packed that evening. The amateur, resplendent in full evening dress, asked Gottschalk to give him a piano near the footlights in full view of the audience, so the dumb instrument was placed centre stage, close to the prompter. Before they appeared, Gottschalk told the thirteen pianists that in order to produce the greatest effect it was essential not to play any preludes, but to surprise the public by at once 'attacking the flourish of trumpets with which the March in *Tannhäuser* commences'.

They began. All went marvellously. 'In the midst of the piece I looked at my amateur: he was superb; he was sweating great drops; he was throwing his eyes carelessly on the audience and performing with miraculous ease the passages apparently the most difficult. His friends were enraptured. They applauded to excess. Some enthusiast even cried out, "Hurrah for –! Encore! Encore!" We must repeat the piece. But at the moment of recommencing, the amateur forgot my instructions not to play any prelude, and could not resist the temptation to play a little dramatic scale. I see him now! The stupor on his countenance . . . He recommenced his scale. Nothing! The piano was mute. For an instant he had the idea that the ardour with which he had played had been fatal to the strings, but, throwing a glance inside, he saw them all right. Without doubt it must be the pedals, so after some shakes impressed on the pedals, he began again his little chromatic scale. Then, persuaded that the piano was just out of order, he strove to make me understand that we could not begin again the March.

'"Pst! Pst!" said he with a wild air, but I had seen the danger, and without loss of time, I had given the signal and the March was recommenced. My young man, to save appearances before the audience, made the pantomime of the passages, but his countenance, which I saw from below, was worth painting. It was a mixture of discouragement and of spite. The fury with which he struck the poor instrument, which could do nothing, was very funny.

'"That was very well done, gentlemen," I said, on entering the artists' room, "but the effect was less than the first time."

'"The mischief!" said my amateur to me. "My piano broke all at once!"

'The secret was kept a long time by my tuner, but it finally leaked out, or at least I had reason for supposing it did from the furious glances that my unfortunate amateur threw on me one day when I happened to salute him on meeting him in the street.'

★

Strads don't dine

★

Musicians in the past have often suffered from the insulting behaviour of those who regard themselves as superior beings. As late as the 1920s, a duchess asked Paderewski to play after a dinner she was giving for King George V and Queen Mary. He asked for a fat fee, which she agreed to pay, adding in her letter, 'Please accept my regrets for not inviting you to the dinner. As a professional artist, you will be more at ease in a nice room where you can rest before the concert.'

The great pianist wrote back: 'Dear Duchess, Thank you for your letter. As you so kindly inform me that I am not obliged to

Pablo Sarasate, Spanish violinist and composer

[131]

be present at your dinner, I shall be satisfied with half of my fee.'

Another pillar of London society sent a note to the Spanish virtuoso, Pablo Sarasate, at his hotel when he arrived in London. This read: 'Dearest Maestro, How lovely to have you back in town. Can you dine with us tomorrow?' A postscript added: 'Please don't forget to bring your Stradivarius.'

Sarasate replied: 'Delighted to see you. I most certainly accept your invitation to dinner tomorrow.' And he too added a PS: 'My Strad does not dine.'

Pasta was
their password

Edouard de Reszke needed large amounts of food because of his size, and his brother Jean had an appetite almost matching his. Often after a dinner of many courses they would go on elsewhere and have a 'snack'. This usually consisted of a dozen large beef sandwiches and four half-bottles of wine, and would be followed by a repeat order. A close friend once commented, 'It was actual hunger, and not the jaded palates of two gourmets dissatisfied with the meal.'

Having lived for several years in Italy, the de Reszkes' favourite cuisine was of that country. 'Why should I fill up on soup?' Edouard complained in St Petersburg. 'A dinner should begin with pasta.' James Huneker occasionally watched the brothers eat their midnight supper after singing at the Met, and he wrote: 'It was a spectacle that would have driven a dyspeptic frantic. The spaghetti was literally wheeled into the room and disappeared like snow under the rays of the sun.'

This passion for pasta was one common to many of the great singers of the Golden Age, as we shall see. At dinner-parties the de Reszkes would keep the company constantly amused by the brilliant way in which they mimicked operas in progress, imitating other singers, the various instruments in the orchestra, even animals. Once at Coombe, Kingston-on-Thames, when dining with their friend Lady de Grey, Jean and Edouard enjoyed themselves so much that they were nearly late for a performance at Covent Garden, missing the train that would have enabled them to reach the opera-house in time. Fortunately the honorary president of the local fire brigade was a guest at the party, and the swiftest horses available bore the brothers up to town aboard Kingston's finest fire-engine, with all bells ringing – and they appeared right on cue.

★
Caruso and the miracle-working chef
★

When Enrico Caruso was in his mid-twenties and poor, he sang with Giuseppe de Luca at the opera-house in Genoa. They liked eating in restaurants, but lack of funds usually prevented their doing so. One evening, however, they dined at Righi, and its owner, noticing the pair, pressed them to sing to his customers. They agreed; Caruso began with the 'Flower Song' from *Carmen*, then de Luca joined him in the popular duet from *The Pearl-Fishers*. The diners were delighted with this unexpected feast of fine singing, and the wily proprietor urged his customers to buy more wine with which to toast the singers, whom he hugged with much show of affectionate admiration. But when they rose to leave, a waiter hurried after them with a piece of paper and the two men stared incredulously at what proved to be a large bill. They asked to see the *padrone*. Surely, they protested, you cannot charge us 180 lire after we have sung to your customers all this while? He merely shrugged and moved away. Caruso and de Luca conferred together, then cornered the proprietor and told him that their normal charge for such a concert was 300 lire: since their meal had cost 180 lire, he owed

Enrico Caruso, in *I Pagliacci*. The great tenor had a
passion for pasta

them 60 lire each. The outwitted restaurateur waved them outside, and took refuge in his den.

When he was in the United States, Caruso missed the cooking of his native land, especially Neapolitan dishes. Knowing this, Philip Crispano of the Met would comb New York for small *trattorie* run by Italian families, where the tenor could relax and have fun. The restaurants he frequented most were Del Pezzo's, famed for its clams, spaghetti and *zabaglione*, and Pane's on West 47th St.

When touring the States, Caruso would make friends with the chefs at hotels where he stayed, so that he could go into their kitchens and supervise the preparation of his pasta. Upstairs in the dining-rooms, *pour épater les bourgeois*, he would deliberately eat like an uninhibited peasant, grimacing as he gloatingly wound huge coils of spaghetti round his fork and pushed them with gusto into his mouth. This clowning would be accompanied by loud exclamations of appreciation, and the more shocked the others around him looked, the happier he would become and the more startling his antics. On one famous occasion he took back with him to the opera-house some sausages to eat during the evening. He was appearing as Rodolfo with Melba as Mimi, and when singing 'Your tiny hand is frozen', he slipped one into her hand. As she dropped it in disgust, he whispered, 'Eengleesh lady no lika da sausage?' Also in *La Bohème*, he once handed Antonio Scotti a raw egg, then squeezed his hand so that it broke.

Hedda Adlon was the daughter-in-law of Lorenz Adlon, who started the celebrated Berlin hotel named after him, of which Escoffier was the first chef and which was destroyed in the Second World War. In her reminiscences, she recalled how Caruso stayed there when singing at the opera-house, accompanied both by a secretary and a personal chef. The latter suddenly invaded the kitchen and announced with flamboyant self-importance that only he must cook for the *maestro*. All the staff gathered round the table allotted to him so that he could prepare what they expected to be gastronomic marvels – but much to their disappointment, after a display of histrionics, all he produced was, as he informed them, 'Mid-day spaghetti. Grand supper this evening!' Then, as though performing some elaborate ritual, he arranged the long strands on a silver dish and placed it on a tray which he carried proudly upstairs to Caruso in his suite. Later, this culinary virtuoso told everyone he met that it was thanks to his way of blending just the right amount of olive oil with his ingredients that the smoothness of Caruso's melodic line was maintained, while a meticulously blended vegetable sauce fortified his vocal chords, and a carefully weighed ration of meat gave his *bel canto* its incomparable lustre.

The great tenor was billed to sing the Duke in *Rigoletto* at a command performance in the opera-house before the Kaiser. On the morning of the day in question, Caruso's thin secretary, looking more lugubrious than usual in his best black suit, raced down to the reception desk and moaned that his employer had a sore throat and was in urgent need of medical attention. The news delighted the house doctor, a forthright and drily sarcastic man named Küttner, who had been complaining that his business at the hotel had been very slack. He found Caruso seated in his suite with a thick woollen scarf round his neck, a shawl about his shoulders, and his hat on his head. The doctor took out a throat-mirror and asked the patient to say 'Ah!' This request, made in German, was not understood, and the secretary instead dashed into the adjoining room and returned with a tuning-fork with which he sounded the note A. In desperation, Dr Küttner seized Caruso by the jaw, forced open his mouth and, not knowing the Italin for 'say', cried: '*Cantare*, maestro! *Cantare* A!'

The tenor's response was instantaneous. Pushing away the other's hand and, sustaining the note as long as his breath held out, he sang a superb high A. This enabled Dr Küttner to peer down his patient's throat, which was almost imperceptibly red. That, and the flawless vocal brilliance, convinced him there was little cause for concern. All the same, such a distinguished artist needed tactful treatment, and he told him in German to keep a cold compress round his throat. The three Italians stared uncomprehendingly at him, so he went into the bathroom and, bringing back a wet towel, held it out to Caruso, indicating in dumb show what he must do. Then, pointing towards the bedroom, Küttner gave the tenor a pat and said in his poor Italian, '*Sera returno.*'

Before the doctor could leave, however, the secretary brandished a newspaper before him and thrusting the tuning-fork at the announcement that Caruso would be singing at the Berlin Opera that evening, he shouted that his employer must be cured well before then. Shaking his head decidedly, Küttner replied, '*Niente cantare! Niente Opera.*' These words enraged the others. The cook waved his fist menacingly at the doctor, who felt sure that if that tuning-fork had been a dagger, the secretary would have stabbed him. '*Nix dottore!*' they shouted. As he retreated into the passage, they added contemptuously, '*Ignorante!*' and slammed the door on him.

It was almost mid-day when the singer's cook hurried down into the hotel kitchen and told its staff that he had thought of a dish that would cure Caruso and enable the command performance to take place. '*Taglioni!*' he cried, and set to work preparing a pasta, rolling it, cutting it into strips, cooking these and giving them a lavish coating of butter and Parmesan cheese – all the time singing arias from *Rigoletto*. Finally, he placed the pasta on a large silver dish, poured thick tomato sauce all over it, and carried his gastronomic cure for a sore throat upstairs to Caruso.

And that evening the command performance took place as arranged, as the *maestro*'s chef had predicted. The critics were unanimous in saying that never had the great tenor been in better form, and cynical Dr Küttner was overheard muttering something to himself about the placebo effect of pasta.

Let us now cross the Atlantic and the American continent to San Francisco and another noted hotel, the Palace, and learn what meat Caruso doted on. In the *Examiner* for 9 April 1905, its distinguished critic Ashton Stevens published an account of an interview he had with him. It reads:

Never again shall I call a tenor haughty or arrogant. At 4.40 of the afternoon of his arrival we met in the Caruso suite at the Palace. It was after six before I could wring myself away . . .

The room was full of talk, talk, talk – Italian, English, now and then an exclamation in French. We sat around a mahogany table, and Caruso said with a great laugh, 'A cocktail, an American cocktail – eh?' He turned to Igoe [Hype Igoe, the *Examiner*'s cartoonist] and said, 'Have a drink?'

'Temperance!' cried the cartoonist.

'I like the temperance, but I like too the little thing to drink, and the macaroni, and – oh, yes! The roast beef. I love the roast beef. I love it too much.' Tenderly he rubbed his palm over the place where the good roast beef belongs, and sighed. 'I sing on roast beef. I am a roast beef singer – only I must eat it at one o'clock.' He placed two palms where one had been before. Fortunately his frock coat swings from a generous chest hung high, and even magnifies his five feet eight inches. He is a thick man from cheek to calf, but as active as his eyes. The very hair of him – black as doom – is active. He is a thick-set specimen of what mothers call 'the dark and dangerous' type . . .

'I sing always' [Stevens reports Caruso as saying later]. 'As a boy I sang in the choir at Naples. As a mechanic I sang as I worked. I serenaded the ladies. One day when I was at work I sang the Litany one hundred times and was given two lire – forty cents. I make a little more money now by not singing so much. . . . I was a boy soprano and my voice failed me at fifteen. But at seventeen I was a tenor. I couldn't go on the stage. I went into the artillery, and my major wanted to know who was that fellow who sang all the time. . . . One day he took me to a friend, a wealthy amateur musician, who listened and taught me the tenor roles in *Cavalleria Rusticana* and *Carmen*. One day I did not sing at all. The major sent for me.

'Why do you not sing today, Caruso?'

'I cannot sing, sir, on greasy soup!'

'Next day my soup was strong and there was no grease on it. But the other soldiers called me the son of the major. Six months later I was making my début in Naples.'

And in Naples during the entr'actes, young Caruso would lower a string from his dressing-room window and draw up sardine and cream-cheese sandwiches which he had persuaded a pal to buy for him. Having been a poor and struggling singer in his youth, he was sympathetic all his life towards those beginning their careers. For example, in New York during the season every Tuesday afternoon just before three o'clock, a special Metropolitan Opera House train would leave Penn Station for Philadelphia, returning after two o'clock next morning; and on the way back Caruso would order supper for the chorus at his expense.

Gigli

Often described as 'Caruso's successor' by the popular press, Beniamino Gigli was born in 1890 in the small Italian town of Recanati. His father struggled for a living, making and mending boots and shoes, and when cheaper factory-produced footwear became popular loss of trade forced him to find other employment as the cathedral's bellringer. Beniamino was not yet aged seven when he joined the boys' choir. He loved singing and did so whenever possible – often he would climb to the top of the belfry and, well above the surrounding roofs, would sing out as loudly as he could. The people called him '*il canarino del campanile*'.

The 'canary' left school when he was twelve and worked for the next five years as an assistant in a chemist's shop, but his growing ambition was to become an opera-singer. Then he became friendly with Giovanni Zerri, a cook from a seminary in Rome which had come with its students to spend summer by the sea at Recanati. Zerri was so impressed by the youth's singing that he persuaded him to come to the capital and there, while working first as another chemist's assistant and later as Countess Spannochi's servant, Gigli had his voice trained. Success first came when he won a competition in Parma, and soon he made a propitious début at the Teatro Costanzi as Faust in Boito's *Mefistofele*.

It was in the same role that Gigli was to triumph when he sang for the first time at the Met on 26 November 1920, receiving 34 curtain calls. Like Caruso, he missed Italian cooking and would go in search of little family restaurants run by immigrants, and would shop downtown in New York's lower East Side where one could buy smoked Parma ham, Parmesan and Gorgonzola, pasta, herbs, olive oil, and those long brittle sticks of bread called *grissini*. Like Caruso, he too suffered from stage fright before concerts, and to calm his nerves would drink copious draughts of tea and tomato juice, and play patience.

Indulgence in food affected Gigli's girth, and after he had been three years at the Met, some critics began making snide references to his 'unromantic figure'. He was nettled into trying to lose weight by drinking only mineral water, eating 'starchless' pasta, and sucking lemons, crates of which he imported from Sicily. In the summer of 1922 he spent three weeks on a diet at Agnano, a spa near Naples, and on returning to New York he decided to devote some time every day to intensive physical exercise.

Gigli describes in his memoirs how he put himself into the hands of H. J. Reilly, a masseur and athletic coach. These 'tortures', as well as keeping him fit, had the further purpose of strengthening his chest and shoulder muscles 'so as to accommodate the demands made on them by the vocal chords, and to curb the expansion of my girth'. He goes on to claim that tenors 'for glandular reasons tend to be short and excessively round', basses to be tall and thin, while baritones, 'nature's favourites', were normal. Since the tenor's role in opera was

Beniamino Gigli, tenor, and Umberto Giordano,
composer: both needed to diet

almost always that of a tragic or romantic hero, tenors were forced to wage a constant battle against this tendency to put on weight.

The *Brooklyn Eagle* had referred to Gigli as looking like a 'well-fed poet' in *Andrea Chénier*, so as he was to appear as Romeo in the autumn season at the Met, Gigli shunned his favourite restaurants and spent the time instead in Reilly's gymnasium. With the object of wearing away that spare tyre round his middle, he was made to lie flat on his stomach in an iron cradle, held fast by a sort of life-belt round his waist. As Reilly pressed an electric button, the cradle would rock purposefully.

Thanks to these efforts, Gigli had lost 20 lbs by the time he first appeared as Romeo at the Met, on 24 November 1922. He knew that many in the audience would remember Jean de Reszke in the role, and also that how ever much he slimmed he could never compete against memories of that most handsome of tenors. No doubt this affected his self-confidence, for in the fourth act he lost his footing on the steps of Juliet's bier and fell awkwardly on the stage, arousing titters. The *New York Sun's* verdict was typical: Gigli had 'failed to convince as a tragic lover'. Nevertheless, the critic thought Gigli had found in Romeo 'a role that indulges all the virtues of his voice'.

Gigli was a close friend of Umberto Giordano, the hero of whose opera *Andrea Chénier* was one of the parts he most enjoyed singing. Giordano was very stout and had an enormous appetite, and when staying with Gigli, he noticed one day at luncheon that his host was dieting.

'I think I'll follow your example,' he remarked. 'I need to lose a little weight myself. That stuff you're eating looks quite good. May I have some too?'

The 'stuff' was a special brand of starch-reduced spaghetti. After quickly disposing of a generous helping of it, Giordano eyed with mounting interest the risotto cooked with mushrooms and white truffles which Gigli's family were eating. He sniffed approvingly. 'Listen, Beniamino,' he said when he could bear the sight no longer, 'your spaghetti was fine, but this looks even better. I think I'll have a mouthful – just to sample it.' His 'mouthful' was followed by the rest of the risotto, piled twice on to his plate. Until the end of his visit, Giordano kept to this 'diet': first he shared the non-fattening spaghetti with Beniamino, then he helped the others to empty the dishes containing their food.

As time passed, Gigli abandoned the struggle to slim and, thanks to his superb voice, this certainly did not diminish his popularity. To show that he regarded the pleasures of the table as essential to happiness, he proudly boasted that in the sumptuous villa he built at Recanati, with its sixty rooms, twenty-three bathrooms, and swimming pool, there was also 'a kitchen large enough to hold food for twenty people for a year'.

—————————— ★ ——————————
Chaliapin and the English breakfast
—————————— ★ ——————————

One of Gigli's close friends was Fedor Chaliapin, the great Russian bass. Unlike the great tenor, Chaliapin was a superb actor who excelled in the art of gesture and who dominated the stage with his presence. As a man he was unpredictable and uninhibited, passionately interested both in food and in women. He stayed at the Savoy Hotel in London when singing at Covent Garden, and, being very particular as to how the bortsch of which he was so fond was prepared, he would go down into the kitchen and supervise its cooking. At a later date, before appearing as Don Quixote, he also was forced to diet, and, as Stanley Jackson so aptly puts it, he would sulk in his suite 'looking like a dehydrated Buddha' and longing for the day when he could consume all the bortsch he wanted. Anything containing chocolate also appealed to him – until his pet monkey, Boris, died from over-eating a rich assortment.

When Gigli and Tauber were also living at the Savoy, they and Chaliapin dined together as often as possible. If in festive mood, they would recruit another singer and march into the restaurant roaring out the Quartet from *Rigoletto*. The trio were great trenchermen, and never tired of discussing various ways of cooking rice and new recipes in which it was the chief ingredient.

For a supper to celebrate a gala performance of *Boris Godunov* starring Chaliapin, the Savoy's *maître chef*, François Latry, prepared a menu that included not only Russian dishes in honour of the bass, but also Italian and Austrian ones as tributes to Gigli and Tauber. Up in Chaliapin's suite after the dinner, the three friends made music till dawn.

Chaliapin once spent a weekend with other guests in a stately home in Lancashire. It was in the days when breakfast was almost a banquet, and the sideboards would be arrayed with dish after dish – grilled kidneys and bacon, lamb cutlets, devilled turkey, fried sole, salmi of game, scrambled eggs, and so on. The bass, however, told his hostess that he never came down to breakfast and preferred just coffee upstairs. Next morning, however, the breakfast aromas wafted up to Chaliapin's bedroom so temptingly that he came down in his dressing-gown, and, picking up not a plate but a large silver tray, helped himself lavishly to everything on display. Then he sat down and, after devouring it all, declared that till that day he had not known that the English breakfast was the finest in the world.

This was indeed praise from a man who always spoke his mind. At a hotel in Sydney, Australia, there is a large grease mark on the wall and a plaque recording the fact that it was made by a goose thrown in anger by Chaliapin because he thought it so badly cooked.

Apart from food, the famous bass also loved many women, and when sitting alone in the Savoy restaurant he would turn the three large rings worn on his fingers as a signal to approaching sweethearts to make themselves scarce, since his wife was expected. Once on tour, the morning after spending the night with a blonde, he promised her, 'I shall give you tickets to hear me sing at the opera tonight.' The girl protested that, being poor, she wanted cash, and added, 'When one is hungry, one needs bread.' To which, he retorted, 'If you want bread, you should have slept with the baker.'

On another occasion Chaliapin was asked by a journalist what kind of women attracted him most, and he replied, 'Those who aren't too thin, have long hair to keep one warm in winter, and are fine cooks.'

Ivor Newton has described how one morning in the 1920s he came across Chaliapin dressed to kill in Monte Carlo. The Russian, who was clad entirely in white from rakish panama to elegant shoes, inquired, 'What are you doing here?', and the pianist explained that he was there to play for Conchita Supervia.

'They tell me she is a very beautiful woman,' remarked Chaliapin.

'She's certainly a very beautiful woman, and what is more she is a very accomplished artist,' Newton responded.

Fedor Chaliapin as Boris Godunov

Chaliapin beamed. 'Well, in that case offer her my *hommage*. And tell her that although I have the voice of a bass, I have the heart of a tenor.'

Newton reported the conversation to Conchita, who said, 'I'm not interested in these Russian fantasies.'

According to Artur Rubinstein, Chaliapin had a very limited recital repertoire and devised a cunning way of concealing this weakness. Instead of printing a programme, he would distribute booklets containing about 500 songs, all numbered, and would simply announce the number of his next song, which the audience would then look up. Rubinstein claimed that he could always guess what Chaliapin would sing: 'It would be "The Two Grenadiers" by Schumann, "The Flea" by Moussorgsky, two songs by Anton Rubinstein, and two or three more, that was all. But the innocent public was amazed by the immense repertoire of the clever fellow.'

The managing director of Monte Carlo Opera once said of Chaliapin, 'There are many learned men who can tell you all about the wonders of the sky. There are other learned professors who could tell you all about the wonders of the deep. But there is no one on this earth who will tell you what that *beau chic* will do in the next half-hour.'

Chaliapin was notorious for feigning ill-health and cancelling performances. He varied his excuses and once, when suffering from mild indigestion through overeating, he told the management he had food-poisoning and could not sing. But the impresario concerned thought of an ingenious way of teaching him a lesson. Chaliapin, in his memoirs, describes what happened. Suddenly his bedroom door burst open and he was confronted by 'a long, bony lady, wearing spectacles, with frowning eyebrows, and a turned-down mouth'. Pointing an aggressive finger at him, she said something in English. 'I gathered she wanted to know if I were Chaliapin . . . With eloquent gestures, she then bade me to lie down on the bed. I did so, and to my horror saw her removing instruments from her bag . . . I saw that I was to have a colonic lavage. This scared me and I yelled for the valet . . . He explained that the lady was a doctor who would cure me within twenty-four hours. I asked him to convey my respects to her, but that I was not requiring her services . . . The instrument for lavage hung in the air. I pleaded with her to go away. "I will sing! I will sing! Just go away. Please!" And she went. The scene made me laugh, and in fact calmed me down a little. Although that night I was feeling exhausted, I sang well.'

Chaliapin first visited New York in 1906 and soon gained a reputation as a gourmet. When he set sail for Europe the following year, he was asked by a reporter what he liked best in their city and his reply was: 'The Castle Cave Restaurant on Seventh Avenue in the Twenties.' This was at the time an unpretentious but homely eating-place, with a friendly chef owner named Bardush. The bass did not return to the States until 1921, and there to meet him as the liner docked was Bardush in the latest model Packard. That night the two men and impresario Sol Hurok feasted until 4 a.m., starting with Bardush's speciality, oysters – of which Chaliapin ate nearly four dozen – followed by giant steaks. Ignoring Prohibition, Bardush produced vintage French wines for this great reunion. Chaliapin had given his restaurant invaluable publicity by that long-ago remark to the reporter, turning it into a gold-mine, and now Bardush was showing his gratitude.

★

Richard Tauber

★

Mention has been made of how Richard Tauber shared with Chaliapin and Gigli a great fondness for rice. Tauber had actually become friendly with Gigli some years earlier when the latter was singing in *Rigoletto*. The word *risotto* was almost a password of affection between them, and among Richard's treasured possessions was a telegram from Gigli sent to him on New Year's Eve, 1931, which read: '*Thanks fuer guten wuenschen risotto today aufwiedersehen.*'

Tauber also kept the menu for the dinner given on board the *Anchises* in his honour when he sailed on her after giving a concert in Sydney in August 1938. It included: *Caviar Glacé Blossom Time – Consommé Heart's Desire – Filet de Sole Sauce*

Pagliacci – *Suprême de Volaille Petite Diana* (named after his wife) – *Côte de Boeuf Braisé Melody of Love* – *Asperges en Branches Tauber* – *Coupe Singing Dream* – *Eclairs Land of Smiles* – and *Sardines à la Cancelled Concert (Diable!)*. A menu of greater importance in Tauber's life was the one taken away from a luncheon table at the Savoy, on the back of which was written the agreement, witnessed by Chaliapin and Franz Lehár, for Tauber to sing in English for the first time.

Both Evelyn Laye and Vera Schwarz who sang with Tauber have described him as being like a child about food. He had only to see his favourite sweet, apricot dumpling, for him to beam with pleasure and order several helpings. When Evelyn Laye appeared with him in the musical *Paganini*, she kept a store of chocolate-bars for him in her dressing-room. 'There would be a tap at the door,' she recalled, 'and a smiling face would appear round the corner. "You have sweets? Oh, thank you, darling *schnappula!*" and grabbing them, he would gaily plant a kiss on the top of my head and vanish to his own dressing-room.'

Tauber once took a serious risk, after he had left Nazi Germany, by slipping across the frontier so as to enjoy his favourite dishes at a celebrated restaurant. Suddenly his companion noticed that storm-troopers at other tables were discussing him, and the pair just managed to escape by slipping out of the back entrance.

Even when critically ill in hospital shortly before he died, Richard's chief interest (apart from music) was still in food. He was asked if there was anything he would like. 'Yes, a large helping of Spaghetti Bolognaise,' he murmured. They brought it to him, and he left nothing of what proved to be his last meal.

Feasting with
nightingales –
and a swan

★

The cook's diva wife,
and the cook's diva daughter

★

The life of a professional singer does not allow much time to learn cooking, so it can be an advantage to marry a cook. Anastasia Robinson, the eighteenth-century contralto who graced Handel's operas, had, according to a contemporary, 'a pleasing modest countenance with large blue eyes', and always behaved like 'a gentlewoman with perfect propriety'. At the age of twenty-six, she retired from the operatic stage on marrying the Earl of Peterborough, who was a superb chef and never happier than when working in the kitchen.

'Those who have dined with him at Parson's Green say that he had a dress for that purpose, like that of a tavern cook,' wrote Dr Charles Burney, 'and that he used to retire from his company an hour before dinner time, and having despatched his culinary affairs would return properly dressed and take his place among them.' But there was, however, another side to his character. An uncontrollable temper made him 'a very awful husband, ill-suited to Lady Peterborough's delicate sentiment'.

One of the most colourful of eighteenth-century prima donnas, Caterina Gabrielli, was the daughter of a Cardinal's cook and for that reason was known as 'La Coghetta'. She had a slight squint in her right eye which gave her a roguish expression, and was the first singer to be called a coloratura. Brydone, the traveller, described her as 'the greatest singer in the world'. When really exerting herself, she sang to the heart and 'her wonderful execution and volubility of voice' had long been the admiration of Italy. She was 'certainly the most dangerous syren of modern times' and had made 'more conquests, I suppose, than any one woman breathing'.

La Coghetta appeared in Vienna from 1754–61, mostly in Gluck's works. The Emperor fell in love with her, and she became rich through his generosity. Gabrielli so excited the passions of the French Ambassador there that he tried to shoot her in a fit of jealousy, and she was saved only by the whalebone in her stays. Eventually banished from the Austrian capital, she went on to triumph in the major opera-houses of Italy, but had to leave each city in turn on account of the duels she provoked among her admirers.

When Brydone first saw her perform in Palermo, she was well over thirty but looked no older than eighteen. When she was in a bad temper, which was often, Gabrielli would only hum her arias, and the best way to induce her to sing them was to persuade her favourite lover of the moment to sit in the centre of the pit or the front box. Roused by desire, 'she would address her tender airs to him and exert herself to the utmost'.

The Viceroy once invited her to a banquet attended by all the nobility in Palermo, but she failed to appear, and he ordered the serving of the meal to be delayed while a messenger hurried off to find out what had happened. He found her reading in bed: her excuse was that she had entirely forgotten the function. Gabrielli's host might have forgiven her for this, had she not sung her part in the opera-house later that evening so very *sotto voce* that the Viceroy and his guests could scarcely hear her. Exasperated by her behaviour, he sent round a message threatening punishment if she did not raise her voice. She replied that he might make her cry but would never make her sing, so he had her confined in prison. There she sang to the prisoners, paid for them to have a fine dinner every day, and distributed large sums of money to the poor ones. This made her so popular that after a fortnight the Viceroy was forced by public agitation to release her, and cheering crowds accompanied her home.

In 1780 La Coghetta retired and went to live in Rome where she maintained the state of a queen. One day a Florentine nobleman visited her and by accident, as he stooped to kiss her hand, one of his lace ruffles caught in a brooch of hers and was torn. She sent him next day six bottles of wine, and in place of corks had the necks stuffed with pieces of the most costly lace.

★
Adelina Patti
★

Adelina Patti, the supreme diva of the last century, also maintained the state of a queen when she retired. 'There is only one Niagara, and there is only one Patti,' declared Jenny Lind to Sir Arthur Sullivan after they had heard her sing at Covent Garden. 'An artist by nature so perfect that perhaps there has never been her equal,' agreed Verdi. When asked to name his three favourite prima donnas, he answered: 'First, Adelina. Second, Adelina. Third, Adelina.'

Born in Madrid in 1843, she went with her parents at the age of three to settle in New York. Four years later, Patti displayed such precocity that, billed as 'The Wonderful Child Prima Donna', she toured the States with the showy Norwegian violinist Ole Bull, and developed such a taste for champagne that when he refused to give her a second glassful she slapped his face.

When she reached her tenth birthday, it was thought wise for Adelina to retire to allow her voice to develop without risk of being strained, and in 1859 she resumed a career that was to see her acclaimed in every major opera-house. As the wife of the

Marquis de Caux, equerry to the Emperor Napoleon III and director of Court cotillions to the Empress Eugénie, she occupied a unique social position – until she eloped with the tenor Ernesto Nicolini, father of five, whom she married after protracted divorce proceedings.

Accustomed to luxurious living, Patti insisted on comfort on stage, too. When playing the title role in *Aida* at its Covent Garden première on 22 June 1876, with Nicolini as her lover Radamès, she instructed the stage manager to leave a swans-down-filled cushion on the stage for her use in the last scene where, as the Egyptian slave-girl, she conceals herself in a dungeon so that she may share Radamès's fate of being buried there alive. Just before the closing duet, 'O terra addio', Adelina placed the cushion behind her, kicked the long train of

Adelina Patti, supreme diva of the nineteenth century

her elegant gown into a decorous position with one Louis XV-heeled satin slipper, and, assisted by the tenor, sank gracefully back and expired.

Escoffier was a great admirer of Patti. She stayed at both the Grand in Monte Carlo and at the Carlton in London during the years when he was their chef, and he named several dishes after her.

Because Nicolini longed to lead the life of an English country gentleman, Adelina bought a mock Gothic castle, Craig-y-nos, beautifully situated in the Swansea valley, and made it her home from 1884 until her death in 1919. There she entertained in queenly style, employing chefs trained and recommended by Escoffier.

⋆

Nellie Melba

⋆

Escoffier was dining at Frascati's with Mme Duchêne, wife of the manager of the Ritz, when she asked him the secret of his success. 'Madame,' he smiled, 'it comes from the fact that my best dishes were created for ladies.' The names of his most memorable creations certainly bear witness to that. Take Melba, for instance: in the spring of 1890, when she was twenty-nine years old and unhappily married, she met the handsome Bourbon Pretender to the French throne, Louis-Philippe Robert, Duc d'Orléans, who was eight years her junior. It was the custom in France for young men of his class to be taught the art of love-making by mature women, and Nellie, exhilarated by his admiration, probably became his mistress. To celebrate her singing Elsa in *Lohengrin* at Covent Garden, she arranged a private dinner party at the Savoy where she was staying. As Philippe would be a guest, she impressed on Escoffier the need for perfection, and suggested *pêches flambées* as the sweet. 'Leave it to me, madame,' he told her.

Nellie Melba, who inspired Escoffier's best-known
creation

The swan which appears in the opera's last scene was Escoffier's inspiration. He had a swan carved out of a block of ice, covered it with spun sugar and set it on a silver dish, with the choicest of fresh peaches resting on a bed of vanilla ice cream between the bird's wings. *Les Pêches au Cygne*, as Escoffier named his creation, delighted Melba and her guests, but the necessity for carving a swan out of ice, using hot irons, chisels, and knives, prevented the sweet from becoming generally popular.

Some eight years later on 1 July 1899, to celebrate the opening of the Carlton Hotel in London's Haymarket, Escoffier prepared another sweet with peaches and vanilla ice cream, but with the addition of puréed fresh raspberries, and told a waiter to set it before Melba, saying that it had been specially made for her. She enjoyed the delicacy so much that she asked its name, and Escoffier sent back the request – would she allow him to call it *Pêches Melba*?

Two years earlier, one Sunday in summer, on the lawn of their house in Golders Green, César Ritz and his wife Marie were entertaining Escoffier to afternoon tea. Marie sighed and, indicating the toast, said that she could never succeed in making it thin enough for her liking. After some discussion, César suggested toasting a slice of bread, cutting it down the middle, and toasting both pieces again. Escoffier went into the kitchen to try out the idea, and returned carrying a plateful of wafer-thin, crisply toasted bread. '*Voici le Toast Marie, après vous, madame,*' he announced. But Marie Ritz did not consider her Christian name appropriate for such a novelty. Shortly after this, Melba confided to Escoffier that she was trying to slim and had been advised by a dietician to feed mostly on dry toast. So the *maître-chef* prepared some as he had done at Golders Green. The diva was delighted with it and readily agreed that it should be called 'Toast Melba'. She had just returned from an American tour, travelling in style in a special Pullman railroad car with her name emblazoned in gold on panels outside, and accompanied by a personal chef and a waiter, whom she dubbed 'Jean' and 'Edouard' after the de Reszkes. Five years later when she sped to Chicago on the famous 'Twentieth Century', a cordon-bleu cook was engaged to prepare on board one of her favourite *plats*: plovers eggs *en croûte* with fresh caviar, which she could not obtain in New York.

With the passage of the years, Dame Nellie became, as Sir Osbert Sitwell aptly put it, 'as fat as an elderly thrush', and when playing Mimi 'with her ample form lying on a couch, she made a surprising and unforgettable type of romantic consumptive'. However, such stoutness could not have been caused by gormandizing, for, if one accepts her memoirs as correct in these matters, her breakfast consisted only of toast and tea, and lunch usually of a cutlet or a little chicken with a light salad and fruit. When singing in the evening, she wrote, her meal at five o'clock consisted of fish, chicken or sweetbreads, a baked apple, and a glass of water.

Melba tried something else in her struggle against excess weight. Clarence Whitehill, the Wagnerian singer, once described how in Chicago in 1899 he visited the diva in her hotel suite. As he walked along the corridor towards it, there was a loud bang and the door ahead shook as if from the impact of a body. '"What sort of roughhouse is going on?" I said to myself. The next moment we were admitted and I had my first glimpse of Melba, a sturdy creature, her hair somewhat dishevelled and flopping over her eyes. She had, when we interrupted her, been wrestling with her conductor, later Sir Landon Ronald. And she had just about pinned him down when we came in.'

Melba always wanted to be ahead of all rivals in whatever she did. The final concert of her last Farewell Tour of Britain ended in Aberdeen with Harold Craxton accompanying her at the piano. She asked him to arrange a supper party to mark the occasion, and this he did, his parting words to the *maître d'hôtel* being, 'On no account is Dame Nellie to see your menu. If she does, she will tear you to pieces.' And he read out: '*Poire Melba*, price 3s; *Poire Tetrazzini*, price 4s.'

★

'The Tuscan Thrush'

★

Much to Melba's annoyance, Luisa Tetrazzini was the only soprano whom Adelina Patti considered worthy to be regarded as her successor. Sir Henry Wood would affectionately refer to

Luisa Tetrazzini: a caricature by Nerman. The 'Tuscan
Thrush' never dieted

her as 'that plump, cheerful little woman, always ready for a
chat'. She was the most generous of divas. Anybody
approaching her with a hard-luck story, however threadbare,
was given money. Once her manager, Signor Tato, chided her
and she replied: 'Poor Tato, but don't you see it makes me
happy? Tato would not like me to lose any happiness, would
Tato?'

The 'Tuscan Thrush' (as some called her) shared a passion
for pasta with her best friend, Caruso. When she sang with him
for the first time, in 1898 in St Petersburg, she longed for
spaghetti and regretted not having brought a supply with her as
Verdi had done when he directed the première of *La Forza del
Destino* there. Later, in New York, Caruso volunteered to make
a special pasta dish for her, and as one of his practical jokes he
used her face powder instead of flour.

Samuel Dickson, in his book *The Streets of San Francisco*, has
described the impression made upon him as a youth when

Tetrazzini triumphed in opera at the old Tivoli there. Sometimes he went with his grandmother to eat in a restaurant, and Tetrazzini would dine at a nearby table. Her meal invariably consisted of *tagliarini* and a carafe of red wine. She ate with relish, smiling happily as she expertly wound as much as she could round her fork and plunged it into her wide mouth, pausing only to wash the food down with a glassful of wine at a time. 'I must not diet,' would be the excuse she made. 'If I diet, my face sag.'

Elsa Maxwell's father was a prominent member of the Bohemian Club, which was then the headquarters in San Francisco for notable visitors, and he brought Tetrazzini to their apartment. Elsa relates that the soprano was flamboyant enough to attract attention in a city 'with a full quota of people studying to be characters', and that she held 'all indoor and outdoor records for collecting love affairs'.

Tetrazzini asked Elsa whether she had a boy-friend. On receiving a negative reply, she cried reproachfully: '*Sensa l'amore, ecco la morte!*' for it was her conviction that without love one might as well be dead. A Senor Urriburri, nephew of the President of Peru, was then, according to Miss Maxwell, a striking proof of the singer's determination to stay alive. She had met the young man in Italy and, abandoning her husband and cancelling all professional engagements, fled with him to America. Unfortunately for her, her husband pursued them and challenged Urriburri to a duel with pistols at dawn.

In her reminiscences, Elsa Maxwell describes how at 8 a.m. on the morning of the duel the ferry-dock at San Francisco was crowded with people waiting to acclaim the survivor – but neither man disembarked from the ferry, or from the next three boats. Could it be that both were dead? Those unable to withstand their curiosity any longer went across the bay to find out, and returned much later reporting no trace of either duellist. The crowd dispersed, and Elsa went to visit Tetrazzini in her hotel. She found her in near-hysterics, but not with grief. There, too, were husband and lover playing cards and drinking toasts to each other's health; they had thought better of it and had called off the duel. Tetrazzini was furious and kept making remarks about men who did not know the meaning of honour, but the reluctant duellists took no notice.

According to Fred Gaisberg, in a different version of this adventure, the husband accepted 'a monetary consolation of some size to resign his claim on the lady'. The original escapade, he claimed, had occurred at an end of opera-season party when Tetrazzini encouraged her conductor-husband to drink until he fell asleep. 'Whereupon she and her lover, a handsome basso, laid him stretched out on the floor, surrounded him with masses of flowers, and, like La Tosca after bumping off Scarpia, placed a lighted candle at each end of him and a crucifix on his breast. Then they eloped together.'

Years later, at the height of Tetrazzini's career, the Savoy would reserve for her Suite 412 overlooking the Thames, which had its own kitchen. There she would make her breakfast with spaghetti as its *pièce de résistance*, and returning late at night with friends after performing at Covent Garden, she would throw off her ermine cloak and start cooking supper. Meanwhile, her star parrot would entertain them by singing 'E' in alt. It was this pet which shrieked disloyally, 'Oh, la, la!', when an inquisitive journalist, interviewing the diva, questioned whether reports were true which claimed that she had been paid a million dollars for her last American tour.

Generous though she was, Tetrazzini's willingness to part with money did not extend to income tax. In May 1920 she was prevented from boarding the *President Wilson*, about to sail from America for Europe, before settling what she owed. Always publicity conscious, she posed before a battery of cameramen handing over the cash to Collector Edwards, and saying with an amiable smile, 'I'm sorry my income tax isn't more, because I love America.'

In London once, when faced with a final demand for £1,500 tax arrears, Tetrazzini invited the inspector to call on her at the Savoy. It was Christmas Eve and when, prepared for battle, the official was ushered into Suite 412 he almost retreated as an explosive sound rang out. But it was only the laughing debtor uncorking a bottle of Bollinger. Pouring out a glassful, she pressed it into his hand while pointing at a table on which were elegantly displayed bundles of crisp new £1 notes, tied with red ribbon. After helping him to count and put them in his attaché case, the diva said, 'There is also room for this,' and added a slice of a rich Christmas cake she had baked in her suite.

Fond as she was of food, Tetrazzini avoided highly spiced dishes and believed that all greasy ones were very bad for the vocal chords.

★

Emma Calvé, diva with four voices

★

Emma Calvé, Melba's one-time rival, was also a pupil of the remarkable Mme Mathilde Marchesi. A wit said that Calvé's beauty lasted longer than her voice whereas in Melba's case the reverse was true. Like Melba, Calvé made her début at the Théâtre de la Monnaie in Brussels, and in her case it was as Marguerite in Gounod's *Faust*. According to Clara Louise Kellogg, the American prima donna, who was present, Calvé's Marguerite was 'a mixture of red pepper and vanilla blancmange.' Also like Melba, she had a sweet named after her by Escoffier.

Emma Calvé's most celebrated role was Carmen. When she appeared in the opera's first performance in French at the Met, critic W. J. Henderson called her 'a creature of unbridled passion with a sensuous, suggestive grace . . . careless of all consequences', while H. E. Krehbiel admitted to being 'magnetized by the frankness of her playing, which would satisfy the most ardent lover of realism'. Later, however, her naturalistic rendering of the role deteriorated into self-conscious exhibitionism, and she became increasingly temperamental. This culminated in a clash at a Sunday evening concert on 24 April 1904, when, about to start singing Provençal songs to conductor

Mottl's piano accompaniment, she asked him to transpose the music a tone lower. He refused, and she walked off the stage of the Met never to return there.

Ivor Newton, who later accompanied Calvé on many occasions, said that she could never decide in which key she could best sing any song, and that 'a sort of allergy prevented her from singing anything in the key in which it had been written'. She would want a song transposed up at one rehearsal and down at the next, but at the concert itself would never sing it in the key he expected. 'My voice is very high tonight,' she would tell him at the last minute. 'You will have to transpose it up.' At the next concert her voice would be 'low', so the same song had to be transposed down. At least, says Newton, she did not achieve anything quite so unusually complex as Clara Butt's demand that he should transpose a song up four tones so that she could sing it an octave below what would have been its true vocal value.

Emma Calvé claimed that she had four voices – dramatic soprano, coloratura, mezzo-soprano, and an uncanny, sexless high tenor taught her by Domenico Mustafà, the highly-regarded castrato-soprano who directed the choir in the Sistine Chapel. Impressed by what she described as 'his exquisite and truly angelic tones', she decided to take some lessons from him. He told her that she would have to practise with her mouth tightly shut for two hours a day, and after ten years she might possibly have acquired the art.

Nevertheless, undaunted, Calvé set to work. Her first efforts were pitiful: 'It sounds like the miaowing of a sick cat,' commented her mother. After only three years, however, Emma had mastered the technique. 'These tones are presumably,' Desmond Shawe-Taylor states, 'the very high floating notes which Calvé could suddenly produce, as though from nowhere, and sustain for an extraordinary duration.' Massenet provided for this fourth voice in his opera *Sapho*, in whose première she sang in 1897. One can also hear her using it in her recordings of the aria 'Charmant oiseau', from David's *La Perle du Brésil*, and of a folksong, 'Ma Lisette'.

Massenet wrote his noisiest opera, *La Navarraise*, for Calvé. The first act opens with a deafening cannonade, and Bernard Shaw, present at the London première, reported that Calvé in the title role made a considerable impact on the audience, 'for before the curtain had been up thirty seconds, during which little more than half a ton of gunpowder can have been consumed, she was a living volcano, wild with anxiety'.

Calvé was not satisfied with this extra voice, and was constantly seeking ways of making her performance more strikingly different from that of other prima donnas. For example, a sculptor, Denys Peuch, told her that he soaked his models' draperies in water before arranging them, so as to obtain graceful lines. This so impressed her that when next she sang Ophelia in Ambroise Thomas's *Hamlet*, she dipped her dress in a basin of water before putting it on for the Mad Scene. The effect was all that could be desired – until the middle of the act. As she lay on a mossy bank beside the lake, playing with her flowers, Calvé noticed that the ballet-dancers around were staring anxiously at her. 'Look – look!' she overheard one whisper, 'what's the matter with her? Why – she's on fire! See that smoke!' But it was only steam coming from her dress, which was drying in the heat generated by the stage lighting. As the dancers became aware of this, they burst out laughing, to the audience's amazement. Calvé caught a bad cold and never repeated the experiment.

Later at the Fenice theatre in Venice, Emma enjoyed a spectacular success in the same role. After the first night she noticed in the wings an elegant little sedan chair which had been specially made for Adelina Patti during her last season there. The diva had refused to travel back to her hotel by gondola at night, fearing that the dampness of the canals might harm her voice, and so she had been carried to and fro in this *portantina*.

'Will the signora be so good as to tell me what she weighs?' the stage manager asked. When told it was nine stone, he went on: 'Splendid! Then you are light enough to use Patti's chair if you wish.'

Calvé was delighted, accepted the offer, and every evening

travelled through the alleys and back to her hotel in this fashion. '*Ecco la prima donna!*' the urchins would shout as they saw the *portantina* appear. 'Here she comes! *E viva! E viva!*'

Emma's last night at the Fenice was a triumph and floral tributes piled up on the stage, so that when the curtain fell for the final time, her mother sent the maid Valerie to call the porters. The two women waited and waited for the maid's return, and at last were about to go in search of her when she burst into the dressing-room, full of apologies and begging forgiveness. She was not unlike her mistress in build and colouring; out of admiration she habitually copied Calvé's walk and gestures; and when wearing a mantilla could be mistaken for her. This the porters had done and as Valerie could speak only French they had not understood her disclaimers and had carried her off. Men had stood cheering and serenading her on both sides all the way – an experience Valerie had clearly relished. When she had reached the hotel, the *padrone* had bowed to the ground before her, then on recognizing the maid had flown into a rage and ordered the porters to hurry back and fetch the real diva. 'They'll get you to the hotel in no time,' Valerie ended. 'The alleys are now empty, and everybody has gone home!'

Calvé's mother, incensed at what had happened, wanted to sack the girl but Emma took it well. But next morning on the hotel bill they found a puzzling extra charge of 200 lire. When her mother summoned the proprietor and demanded an explanation, he replied that it was an old custom, begun by Mme Patti's business manager, to hire the services of waiters and other hotel staff on the last night at the Fenice, and for them to line the route and cheer. He had been certain that Mme Emma Calvé, too, would have wished to ensure that she had people acclaiming her. He was sorry if they were displeased. 'It's really too much,' wailed mother when alone with the diva, 'to have to pay such a price for the glorification of a maid.'

Emma's mother disliked parting with money for they had been very hard up when her daughter was young. This had made success difficult to achieve at the Opéra-Comique in

Paris, where singers had to pay, in cash or sexual favours, to obtain a début. It had taken Emma some time to earn the 30,000 francs charged for her début in *Carmen*, there being a sliding scale according to the opera and the role.

As a girl Emma was so poor that she was unable to afford transport and had to walk many kilometres every day to and from her singing lessons, often in the rain or snow. Impressed by her voice but worried by her frail appearance, a next-door butcher in Montmartre, where the Calvés lived, insisted on providing her with beefsteaks and cutlets, not to be paid for until she had made her name.

Calvé's whole attitude to the relationship between eating and drinking and her art is graphically given in the account, contained in her memoirs, of a visit to sing at Bayreuth, arranged by the great conductor Hans Richter. On arrival at Wahnfried, she found that Wagner's widow Cosima had become prejudiced against her because of the denigrations of some unfriendly artists. As a result, Cosima merely asked Calvé to sing at an evening party the next night, an invitation which she did not dare refuse although she had not come all that distance only to sing at a *soirée*.

On entering the drawing-room, Calvé reported that she was shocked with everything she saw and heard, for there was nothing at all attractive about the décor and the furnishings. 'I, who have always been specially sensitive to these things, felt morally discouraged at the sight.' Cosima nevertheless greeted Emma amiably, and after she had sung Liszt's *Lörelei* the widow's enthusiasm 'knew no bounds'. But Calvé felt this was due not so much to her singing as to her having chosen a piece by Cosima's father. When the visitor sang her second song, some of the people present stole out of the room 'to fetch, this one a bun, that one a large piece of cake, a third a huge sandwich, and they were devouring their dainties, each with a glass of beer in the other hand, as they listened to my singing, in the corridor opposite the piano, a thing which absolutely took my senses away, and it was only by sheer self-control that I did not stop in the middle of my song and walk out.'

After Calvé had finished, Siegfried Wagner 'wiping the last drop of beer from his moustache, and still eating the end of his sandwich, mumbled to me several compliments, and looking into his fat, uninteresting face I could not help thinking that really great geniuses should not marry and leave wives and children behind . . .'

Calvé continues that, 'speaking of Siegfried's beer', she must give vent to her feelings concerning food and music.

To begin with, I had very queer ideas from my childhood about the material part of our life. I was of an exalted poetical nature, and felt easily upset by things seen and heard. To sit down at meals, to invite people to assemble around a table for the purpose of swallowing and digesting, seemed to me absolutely shocking. That we should hide ourselves while performing this necessity of life, everyone eating in a dark, hidden corner, seemed to me the right thing. The beautiful ladies' head-dresses, garments, and jewels did not seem to be able to disguise the hideous fact that, animal-like, they were enjoying their food. Although to-day I myself heartily enjoy having meals in good company and love to entertain, I always keep my secret thought that the animal life of men should be hidden as much as possible, and that we shall only be civilized when food will be taken in secret and silence.

When Emma Calvé had reached the peak of her fame she went back to Décazeville, the tiny town in the south of France where she had been born. The Mayor rang the tocsin, summoned the peasants from their work in the fields, and had them all gathered together outside the *hôtel de ville*. Then he addressed them: 'I have brought you here to listen to a little nightingale who was born in these parts, flew away, and has now returned. It will sing to you from this balcony. Listen well and I am sure you will acclaim our accomplished *citoyenne*, Mlle Emma Calvé.'

The diva sang to them a selection of the arias that had won her international admiration, but they listened in complete silence. Amazed and distressed, she went down and approached an old shepherd she had known as a child. 'Blaise, what's the matter?' she asked. 'Why didn't you clap or cheer? Did I sing as badly as all that?' The old man, like the others in the crowd, had never heard an opera-singer before and could scarcely conceal his emotion. 'Poor girl, poor girl,' he quavered. 'How you scream! How it must hurt you! You are wearing out your life! Such a waste of strength. It's dreadful!'

★
The 'Butterfly' cook
★

Emmy Destinn, born Kittl in Prague, took her stage name from that of a singing teacher, Destinnovà. Offstage, people often assumed from her appearance that she was a cook, an occupation which, as a girl, she had toyed with the idea of taking up. In 1905 she appeared in the Covent Garden première of *Madam Butterfly* with Caruso as Pinkerton – a part to which, with his short legs and rotund body encased in a too-tight uniform, he was no more suited physically than she to that of a fifteen-year-old geisha. But their singing stirred audiences to frenzied enthusiasm, making them oblivious of the pair's visual shortcomings. Destinn established herself with English critics as the greatest Butterfly of her time.

Earlier that season, Destinn had won acclaim in London for her superb Aida, a role in which she made her triumphant New York début on 16 November 1908 with Caruso as Radamès and Toscanini conducting. The sincerest compliments come from rivals, and Frances Alda wrote in her memoirs that no one in her time sang Aida or Butterfly to compare with Destinn. 'Of course she was stout . . . but her voice so divine like drops of water – and the pathos she put into the role . . . All that made her unforgettable.'

Destinn did not mind being taken for a cook, as she was in fact an excellent one who thoroughly enjoyed giving dinner-parties. She prepared every dish herself in the manner of her native Bohemia, and the meal had not only several courses, but many editions of each one – varieties of both fish and fowl, often six different kinds of meat, and pastries at the end which would have won gold medals at confectioners' exhibitions.

Destinn rarely invited star singers to these feasts, preferring instead to give pleasure to those neglected by Fortune, such as supporting singers, choristers, backstage staff, and students. In their old age many remembered these happy occasions and said that never in their lives had they eaten so well, praising also her thoughtfulness in setting beside every cover some useful gift such as a pair of warm gloves.

Artur Rubinstein, in his reminscences, reveals another facet of Destinn's character. She once invited him for supper in her suite at the Hotel Regina in New York, at which she wore an evening gown slit nearly up to the waist. To his great fright he saw the threatening head of a serpent on her thigh. Looking closer, he found that she had a brightly coloured tattoo of a boa encircling her leg from the ankle to the upper thigh. 'It took me some time to get over the shock. I am afraid I was not at my best that night. Later, she became quite mellow and maternal.'

Rubinstein had to leave next day for London. 'For weeks, she sent me letters in the form of poems . . ., in a fine calligraphy on a special de luxe paper, like a romantic teenager.'

Emmy Destinn: cook, as well as diva

★
Alda – 'The more pounds, the more power'
★

Frances Alda, Giulio Gatti-Casazza's wife, published her reminiscences in 1930 on quitting the Met after twenty-two seasons there. She had never spared herself, having once, for example, sung fifty-two Manons and seventy-four Marguerites in ten months. Food, she wrote, played an important part in giving her the necessary stamina. At the start of her career in Brussels, she would breakfast on porridge, kippers, toast, marmalade, and tea. 'We believed singers needed to eat in those days. If one put on weight – and this one did – well, the more pounds, the more power.' After such a meal she would walk in the park, then practise for an hour with an accompanist from the opera. This would rouse real pangs of hunger, which she would assuage by washing down a dozen oysters with a bottle of stout. By then, it would be mid-day, and she would go for a drive to give her an appetite for lunch at 1.30, when her favourite dish (if she was not singing in the evening) was *waterzooi Gantoise*, a stew of chicken and vegetables in a very rich sauce.

If performing at night, Alda would always lunch on *Boeuf Tartare*. According to legend, this was the dish that the Tartars made their staple diet and that gave them the strength to ravage Asia and Eastern Europe. She made this herself by chopping a raw onion very finely, forming it into a nest for a mound of half a pound of raw minced beef, into a little hollow of which she dropped a raw egg. After garnishing the whole with capers and pouring four tablespoons of olive oil over it, she would eat it, uncooked.

This Frances Alda strongly recommended to all who wanted to achieve diva status, saying: 'After that, if you can't make your voice heard to the topmost seat in the gallery and out into the square before the opera house, you had better stick to radio that furnishes mechanical amplifiers.'

Frances Alda: a glorious voice and an enormous appetite

★

Mary Garden

★

Attracting the attention of the audience to oneself and away from the other artists on the stage is quite an art. Robert Helpmann revealed that he achieved this at the start of his career by putting vaseline on his black hair and then paraffin on top of that. This made his locks glow like polished ebony, drawing all eyes to them.

Mary Garden gained the reputation of being the most expert scene-stealer on the operatic stage, and some of her rivals even accused her of using animals to help her. Those present when she triumphed in the title role of Massenet's *Le Jongleur de Notre-Dame* at Oscar Hammerstein's Manhattan Opera House in 1908, noticed that the donkey appearing with her always pricked up its ears when she sang but looked dejected whenever anyone else did. The creature may, of course, have been genuinely entranced by the sound of Mary Garden's voice, but cynics thought it more likely that she had trained the animal to regard her singing as a signal that it would be rewarded offstage with a particularly toothsome carrot. There were some in the audience who only came to the opera in order to admire this musical donkey.

Gary O'Connor, in *The Pursuit of Perfection*, described Mary Garden as 'a voracious man-eater always boasting of her conquests, but at heart frigid, with lesbian tendencies'. It has also been said that she made a cult of her figure. The Scottish-born prima donna wrote in her memoirs that she never allowed fat to grow on her body and would weigh herself every Sunday morning. 'If I saw a fraction of weight more, that fraction went by the following Sunday.' When she was singing in opera, she achieved this through diet, for she never exercised or took a step that she did not have to take on the day of a performance. But when on vacation she made up for it by swimming and playing as much golf and tennis as possible.

Mary rarely went to dinners. When invited, she would ask if

she might come after the meal, since eating and drinking bored her. She limited her breakfast to two cups of *café-au-lait*, and for lunch liked shellfish (but no other sort of fish), eggs, and everything that came from inside an animal – nothing from its outside except oxtail, which she 'adored'. On returning home at night, and after a hot bath, she would drink a large glass of hot milk with ten drops of iodine in it, which early in her career a doctor in Paris had prescribed as the best reviver after any great exertion and the most efficacious for toning up the nervous system.

That such a frugal eater should have inspired Escoffier to create a rich dessert and name it after her is surprising, but no doubt Mary Garden appreciated the compliment thus paid her. For Melba, he chose the peach; for Garden, the pear.

★

'The Lily of the North'

★

Lillian Nordica, the American soprano born 'Norton', took the stage name of 'Giglia Nordica' – 'Lily of the North' – at her Italian singing-teacher's suggestion, because of the hostility to such work of the girl's Puritan relations. Even her father was not allowed to bring home his violin which was regarded as the devil's instrument. Nordica was so thin at the start of her career that after lessons in the New England Conservatory she would squeeze through the grating separating it from the concert hall and listen to rehearsals and performances which otherwise, owing to lack of money, she could not have heard.

Following her début at La Scala in 1879, Nordica appeared in Italian and French opera, singing its florid music brilliantly. Then she turned to Wagner, and was the first American to sing at Bayreuth where her Elsa in *Lohengrin* was acclaimed. After 1895, she added Isolde, Brünnhilde, and Venus to her repertoire, and triumphed at the Met, where she came to be regarded as the greatest singer of these roles.

According to Blanche Marchesi, Nordica was 'a slow study' but stubbornly industrious, and she underwent 'the torture of one thousand piano rehearsals' before she ventured to sing Isolde. At the last of these, her faithful French accompanist became so enthusiastic that he tried to kiss her, but she dodged him and ran out of the room. She told Blanche about her experience, expressing horror at the very thought of the man's lips touching hers. When the other asked why that should have upset her so much, she replied, 'He had been eating garlic.'

Among Nordica's admirers was Willy Schutz, brother of Felia Litvinne, the blonde and very stout soprano who sang Isolde to Jean de Reszke's Tristan and who had such a taste for chocolates that she would empty a 2 lb box in an evening. James Gibbons Huneker, the American critic, was in Schutz's company on the terrace of the Café Montperino in Paris when the unexpected news reached them that Nordica had married an Hungarian tenor. Willy was heartbroken. He had her pet poodle shipped over from New York: Huneker says it was a fetish for him. The diva's disconsolate admirer and the dog vanished for a week, and when they reappeared the poodle, which had been snow-white, was dyed black, and round its neck it wore a huge crêpe bow, with a smaller piece tied to its tail. The cocottes outside the café set up a wail of commiseration at the sight. 'Oh, *pauvre* Toutou, he has lost his *maman!*' That night Willy Schutz was a hero who had been jilted by a heartless coquette. He sobbed as he looked at the poodle in mourning, but the creature did not seem to mind.

Like Lilli Lehmann's, Nordica's voice was at first a bird-like soprano and, like Lehmann too, she kept her capacity to undertake lyric roles with or without coloratura throughout the time she was singing major Wagnerian parts, when (wrote the critic Henry T. Finck) 'the biggest orchestra could not submerge [her voice] in its tidal waves of sound'. Finck claimed she proved that singing Wagner properly strengthened and beautified the voice: Nordica certainly rarely rested it and once gave a hundred concerts in twenty-eight weeks – a record. To achieve this she practically lived on the railroads, travelling in her own coach, named 'The Brünnhilde', which contained a luxurious drawing-room, a music-room, three bedrooms, a kitchen, and quarters for her servants. Success made her autocratic and outspoken: she once told the Boston Symphony Orchestra that they played 'like a Kalamazoo band'.

Nordica was an excellent cook. After her third husband lost most of her money speculating on Wall Street she had a nervous breakdown, from which she recovered through gormandizing. The result, says Huneker, was that she resembled 'a large, heavily upholstered couch'.

★
The Beauty and the Beast
★

'She was a butterscotch sundae of a woman, as beautiful as a tulip of beer with a high white collar,' wrote A. J. Liebling of Lillian Russell. 'If a Western millionaire, one of the Hearst or Mackay kind, could have given an architect carte blanche to design him a woman, she would have looked like Lillian. She was San Simeon in corsets.' She also ate a fourteen-course dinner almost every night for years, and a popular dessert called after her consisted of half a cantaloupe holding nearly a quart of ice cream.

It was when she heard *Mignon* in her teens that Lillian's ambition became to sing in grand opera. Instead, following lessons from Dr Leopold Damrosch in New York, she joined the chorus of *HMS Pinafore*, married the conductor and was soon divorced. After making her name in Tony Pastor's burlesque of *Patience*, she played the lead in a legitimate production of the same comic opera, followed by a role in *The Sorcerer*, and then, in August 1888, she appeared wearing tights in *The Queen's Mate* at the Broadway Theatre. She objected to dressing like that on tour, but not on account of moral scruples: it was because she feared the ill-effects on her voice of frequent colds caught in draughty theatres. Manager James Duff would not allow her to refuse to wear tights without a drastic cut in her salary, so she fought him in the courts and won not only the verdict but valuable front-page publicity.

Lillian's victory led to Rudolph Aronson's engaging her to star at the Casino. She was now being coached by Louisa Cappiani, the foremost operatic teacher in the States, who on the first night was so carried away by the vocal range and ease of her pupil that at the end she hurled a huge bouquet at her with such force and poor aim that she knocked out the producer instead.

Soon Lillian was enjoying spectacular success and being called America's Queen of Comic Opera. She longed to sing at the Met, but never managed to persuade its board to overcome their prejudice against those they regarded as mere musical-comedy singers. During a courtesy call to Lillian's dressing-room, Melba congratulated her on the brilliance of her high Cs. 'By the way,' she enquired, 'have you ever counted how many times you reach high C at each performance?'

'Eight times, and I give seven performances a week,' boasted Lillian. 'That's fifty-six high Cs a week, not count-ing my practice hours at home each morning. Not bad, is it Nellie?'

Melba shuddered. 'Not bad? It's outrageous! No grand-opera soprano would dream of singing fifty-six high Cs each week! The public never values anything that comes to them so cheaply. Take my advice: give them just two high Cs every night and you'll be far more appreciated.'

'You're right, of course,' Lillian admitted. Nevertheless she went on squandering her vocal riches as before. She married again but the match did not last long, for her new husband was arrested when they were in London and proved to be a bigam-ist. Back in New York, she created the title role in *Princess Nicotine*, in which her leading man was a conceited, handsome *tenor robusti* called Giovanni Perugini – really an American, born Jack Chatterton. The *Dramatic Mirror* reported: 'Until last week, Lillian Russell had it all to herself in the way of stunning costume at the Casino . . . But now all is changed. It is Signor Don Giovanni Perugini who divides attention with Miss Russell. The three costumes he wears are marvels of color. His wedding dress, which is white, with gold clocks running up his stockings, is especially brilliant.'

Perugini made love to Lillian on the stage with tremendous panache. She was enchanted, and when he proposed their marriage she wedded him as soon as possible. George W. Lederer, who attended the civil ceremony, has described what happened when they went afterwards to the Russell residence: 'We had a jolly little supper and then somewhat to my astonishment, since it was hardly the gesture of a bride on her wedding night, the fair Lillian suggested that we all sat down to a game of cards. It was now about 1.30 a.m. We got out cards and chips and presently were in the midst of a friendly little game of poker. An hour later, Perugini got sleepy and retired. But though I made several suggestions that we stop the game, the beautiful Lillian insisted that we continue. She loved cards, and they were her favourite pastime. We kept on playing, playing, playing. I began to think that our hostess' habitual politeness prevented her from getting rid of us, so I suggested to her, as politely as I could, that she boot us out bodily. Whereupon she looked at me very sweetly and said: "Not at all! I wouldn't think of it! I *always* play cards on my wedding night."'

When at last the party ended and Lillian joined Giovanni in their bedroom, he told her: 'I love you too much to defile you.' The marriage was never consummated and he admitted that his purpose in marrying her was to further his own career. There was row after row, and when after two months he tried to throw her out of the window of a seventh-floor apartment, she started proceedings for divorce. Perugini complained tearfully to a reporter: 'Do you know what she did to me? Why, sir, she took all the pillows. She used my rouge – misplaced my manicure set – stole my special handkerchief perfume and put it in her bath . . . Once she threatened to spank me, and she did – with a hairbrush, too. You can't expect a fellow to take a spanking with equanimity, can you?'

Louisa Eldridge, the actress, commented: 'Just think of it! Her first husband, Harry Braham, was an orchestra conductor, her second, Teddy Solomons, was an opera composer, and this one is a tenor. If she only keeps on divorcing and remarrying and can get a basso, she will have her own opera outfit complete.'

After this experience, Lillian waited some years before marrying a fourth husband. Many were the rejected admirers who watched dejectedly when she arrived in fashionable restaurants. Martin's, it was said, was the best showcase for feminine beauty, with its small band of Hungarian gypsies ready in return for a good tip to meet a lady as she arrived and play soft music to her as she moved along the centre aisle to her table. Lillian would enter like a queen and proceed to the sounds of 'When Chloe Sings A Song' or 'Come Down Ma Evenin' Star'.

As Henry Collins Brown has written in *Brownstone Fronts*, a celebrated feature of after-theatre life in New York at that time were the 'bird and bottle' suppers with musical stars. The witching hour was eleven-thirty, when they began to sail in from various Broadway successes, choosing just the right moment for their appearance with costly pearl dog-collars well displayed, and guarded by some proud escort. The orchestra leader would signal to his men to greet each one with the strains of her most popular song. 'She was always just so surprised, fluttered nervously with the great bouquets of violets or orchids which her well-repaid admirer carried for her.'

Always inclined to plumpness, Lillian's figure grew increasingly round as a result of her indulgence in fourteen-course dinners with her best friend for forty years, Diamond Jim Brady – but this did not matter as long as the hour-glass figure stayed firmly in fashion. When the Beauty and the Beast (as they were called) dined together, the fare ordered at Rector's would normally include six dozen oysters, a dozen and a half hard-shell crabs, several lobsters, two steaks, and a large tray of pastries, followed by coffee. She was the only woman ever able to eat as much as he did at one sitting. When the Chicago Exhibition was held in 1893, Lillian sang arias from *La Cigale* and *Giroflée-Girofla* at the Columbian Theatre. Afterwards, the Beauty accompanied the Beast to his favourite restaurant, and as it was the corn season they consumed all they could. Other diners watched incredulously as the waiters carried to them tray after tray laden with corn on the cob soaked in butter, corn sautéd in thick cream, corn fritters, corn chowder, corn pudding, and corn muffins.

But the time came when the press dared to make jests about the Beauty's stoutness. So, one day looking at her reflection in a long mirror after removing her corset, she decided to take drastic action. Bicycling was becoming popular with her sex; women of all ages, shapes, and sizes sent pedestrians scurrying for safety as they sped along the paths in Central Park. So Lillian joined them, wearing an all-white serge ensemble of knickerbockers, gaiters, jacket with huge leg-o'-mutton sleeves, and Robin Hood hat. Her friend the actress Marie Dressler accompanied her, and wrote later: 'Every morning, rain or shine, we would climb on our wheels and, bending low over the handlebars, give an imitation of two plump girls going somewhere in a hurry.'

Lillian proudly told Diamond Jim Brady that her scales showed she had lost several pounds, so he decided to go pedalling, too, and had a number of gold-plated machines manufactured, as well as a special model for her with jewel-studded hubs and spokes and with her initials in diamonds and emeralds inset on the mother-of-pearl handlebars.

The tandem was then the rage, and so as to upstage everyone else Brady ordered a three-seater on which, glittering with diamonds, he sat in front with Lillian behind him and another friend at the rear. His henchman, Dick Barton, would follow on another tandem in charge of the Beast's indispensable orange juice, kept ice-cold in a monster can. Every Sunday when Lillian was in New York they met and went whizzing round the Park to the sightseers' delight and, when necessary, preceded

by policemen on bicycles frantically blowing whistles to warn
the crowds not to obstruct the way. So that their own machines
should always be in perfect condition, Diamond Jim sent them
every fortnight to the electroplater to receive a fresh gloss of
gold. Lillian's bicycle cost $10,000 and, when not in use, was
kept in a plush-lined, custom-made, leather case with her name
painted on it in decorative white capitals. It went everywhere
with her on tour, and the spectacle of her in the saddle attracted
crowds and much profitable publicity.

But although the Beauty and the Beast cared for cycling, they
cared for food far more, and the temptation to resume those
fourteen-course dinners was too great. Lillian now weighed just
under twelve stone. Although the new idols worshipped on
Broadway were seven-stone Anna Held and petite Edna May,
there were still some who regarded as classically perfect the
hour-glass figure that Lillian maintained with the aid of corsets.
At least when she had to sing in the evening, Lillian waited until
midnight before eating a large meal and rationed herself to just a
light repast of up to seven courses at 4 p.m.

The critics, however, criticized Lillian's figure increasingly,
and when she appeared as the prima donna in Offenbach's *La
Belle Hélène* on 11 January 1899, the *New York Journal* commented: 'Lillian has no beauty below the chin . . . she moves
her grand-opera amplitude with the soft heaviness of a nice
white elephant.'

But the Beauty did not care. Jacques Bustanaby, in an
interview published in *Candide*, referred to the days when he
and his two brothers were running the Café des Beaux Arts at
40th St and 6th Avenue, and when Diamond Jim bet Lillian
that he could eat more than she. 'If she could match him, he said
he would give her a huge diamond ring the next day,' Jacques
recalled, and went on: 'Lil slipped out to the ladies' room and
came out with a heavy bundle under her arm, wrapped up in a
tablecloth. . . . She told me to keep it for her until the next day.
"But do not look," she told me. And then she went back to the
table and ate plate-for-plate with big Diamond Jim Brady . . .
and she beat him fair and square. . . . That bundle? What was

in it? Yes, I wanted to know, too. The curiosity of a Frenchman could not stand it. So I looked to see what Lillian Russell had handed me before she went back to out-eat Mr Brady. It was her corsets!'

For some years in the early 1900s Lillian rented Cedar Hall, a large mansion at Far Rockaway, Long Island, from spring until autumn. Cycling had made her an exercise enthusiast and all her guests were pressured into taking some form of it, either in an outdoor gymnasium run by a physical-culture expert or by playing tennis, riding, or, of course, cycling.

Apart from this, Lillian urged her visitors to feed on a plentiful mixed diet supplemented in spring by chopped raw onions at every main meal. She condemned the use of cosmetics, except very sparingly, telling a reporter: 'A woman can gain a fine healthy colour from the use of dyes just about as effectively as she could gain a graceful carriage by rubbing her body with axle grease.'

★

'The only prima donna who eats potatoes'

★

Maria Jeritza, famed for her flamboyant Tosca and fierce Fedora, was an excellent cook. In her memoirs she paid tribute to her mother for having seen to it that when she was a girl she learned to become as proficient in the culinary art as in all the other subjects taught her. 'Your husband shall never have a chance to tell me that you should have gone to cooking school,' Maria quotes her mother as saying.

According to the diva, cooking is quite as great an art 'as impersonating a horrible character in an ultra-modern opera, and it is certainly far more soothing to the nerves and conducive to comfort and happiness'. She adds that before the First World War she employed a young woman who showed promise as a cook, and so she arranged for her to work in the kitchens of the

Imperial Viennese household and to be thoroughly trained in its gastronomic traditions. 'In hundreds of years, the Viennese Court had been famous for the variety and excellence of the dishes served at its tables. When my cook came back to me, she brought with her the choicest of these Court recipes – they actually make one's mouth water – and when I wish to rise to artistic heights in cooking, I always turn to the pages of one of the three fat books of recipes (in French, the official Court language) which I have at home.'

In November 1929, when interviewed by a New York journalist, Jeritza said, 'I believe I am the only prima donna in the world who eats potatoes. I love them *sautées*.' In her opinion, 'Eating has but little to do with the vocal chords, and singers must have food which is tasty as well as nourishing, for otherwise their dispositions suffer and, as a consequence, their performances.'

Maria Jeritza describes Fedora as one of the most exciting roles she ever studied – a real 'black and blue' one because in the excitement of playing his dramatic part the male singer often acted too realistically when he had to grip or hit the soprano. Once in *Der Rosenkavalier* she was struck on the knee-cap, causing her such pain that she almost fell down. When she played Tosca with Scotti as Scarpia, he once asked her why she kept as far away from him as possible and she explained it was through having had more than her share of being buffeted.

Whilst she considered Giovanni Martinelli to be the ideal Count Loris in *Fedora*, Jeritza nevertheless found him as bad a buffeter as the others. In 1923, during the opera's triumphant Met première, he so lived his part that her arm became black-striped as a zebra through his mauling of her. Fortunately, whilst on the stage, she says, she seldom felt any pain because of being so involved in the character. (Something similar occurred at a rehearsal once when she arrived suffering from a stiff neck and Martinelli from a severe attack of lumbago – within a short while these physical ills were forgotten, and when they broke for lunch she exclaimed in astonishment, 'Why I can move my neck!' and Martinelli added, 'And I have no more lumbago!'

Jeritza comments: 'Who could deny the therapeutic power of music and acting after such an experience?')

Some two years later, on 14 January 1925, when *Fedora* was revived at the Met and, owing to the sudden illness of Martinelli, Gigli took over the part of Count Loris Ipanov, Jeritza rebelled and turned the tables on her new tenor. On the opening night she flung herself at him with such ferocity at the close of the second act that he might have fallen had he not supported himself against the scenery. At the next performance she writhed like a hooked fish as he clasped her against his chest in what was intended to be a loving embrace: this resulted in his being sent reeling across the stage, and the audience roared with laughter.

In his reminiscences, Gigli relates how on another evening, during the same act, when he accidentally dropped his top hat, Jeritza deliberately kicked it so that it almost tumbled into the orchestra pit. But on 26 January, towards the final curtain, he had his revenge. They had reached the point where Count Loris finds out that Fedora is a spy. Gigli claims that he could not say for certain what happened then – he might have misjudged the force needed to push her away from him, he might have given way to his pent-up irritation over her past conduct, or she might herself have slipped. However, those watching in the stalls were alarmed to see her stagger away from him and collapse on to the footlights, scraping her legs on the metal and glass.

Gigli hurried to her assistance, but she waved him away and, rising, resumed singing – at a distance. As the scene ended, she ran weeping into the wings, and he followed, apologizing. But she screamed, 'Go away! You wanted to kill me! Murderer! Murderer!'

'Nonsense!' he returned.

'Listen to him!' she interrupted. 'First he tries to murder me, then he insults me.' She clutched at her husband, Baron Leopold von Popper, a tall Austrian army officer who was always on call backstage. 'Defend my honour!' she ordered. 'Challenge that creature to a duel!'

Fortunately for Gigli, the Baron was a reasonable man and he ignored his wife's command. Next day, however, the affair was front-page news and Gigli was forced to issue a statement that it had all been an accident. New York's operatic world ranged itself in opposing camps and the controversy developed into an acrimonious debate about which of them was the Met's leading artist. Jeritza told the Met's general manager that she would never again sing on the same stage as Gigli, but Gatti-Casazza, accustomed to dealing with difficult singers, pointed out that both of them had contracted to appear together in *Tosca* in a fortnight's time, that to break such an agreement would prove very costly to her, and that she would not surely disappoint her adoring public.

On the night, Gigli as Cavaradossi took every care not to upset Jeritza, and there was no trouble until after the curtain had fallen at the end. Going on to the stage, he noticed that she remained in the wings and signalled for her to join him; she ignored this, so he took his bow alone, then made for his dressing-room so that she could take hers without him. Instead, however, Jeritza burst into tears and, despite all the shouts from the audience, stayed where she was. Between sobs she complained that Gigli had tried to steal her glory and that he should have waited to take his bow until she had been acclaimed on her own. Twice the curtain rose and fell without her appearing, then people started to leave. But her supporters went on clamouring for her with mounting insistence.

A quarter of an hour passed, and at last Giuseppe Bamboschek, the leader of the orchestra, went backstage, took hold of her gently but firmly, and led her out in front of the curtain. Her claque shook the building with their salvos. She raised a hand indicating that she wished to speak. 'Gigli not nice to me!' she told them; then, like a tragedy queen overcome by her sorrows, she sank into Bamboschek's arms. Back in her dressing-room, she became hysterical. The Baron, apparently unable to cope, had vanished, so the conductor in desperation telephoned Gatti-Casazza who was in bed at home, asleep. Returning to the opera-house in a taxi, he spent some two hours trying to calm the affronted diva. 'All right,' he conceded at last, 'I'll never ask you to sing with him again.' And Gigli was enormously relieved when he heard the welcome news.

Maria Jeritza enjoyed a much happer relationship with Leo Slezak, a native of Brünn in Czechoslovakia where she was also born. He used to say that he would rather perform with her than any other prima donna, and one day he told her it was because she was so thin. 'I can actually embrace you on the stage when an embrace is in order. I cannot embrace stout prima donnas very well because I am so fat myself!' That stoutness caused an awkward incident once when they were singing side by side in Halévy's *La Juive*. He was standing with his arm about her when suddenly his waistcoat burst under the strain of his deep breathing. In a whisper he begged her to stand as close to him as possible so that it would not be noticed by the audience.

Maria was very proud of her beautiful blonde hair, and when she played the Sicilian peasant girl Santuzza in *Cavalleria Rusticana* the producer had difficulty in persuading her to wear a brown wig. Nanette Guilford was singing Nedda in *I Pagliacci* the same evening, and when Jeritza heard that she would not be using anything to conceal her fair locks she went into her dressing-room and cried, 'You can't wear your own hair!'

'Why not? I can be a northern Italian just as easily as a southern one,' Nanette says she replied. But Maria would not hear of it. 'I've got just the thing for you – and it's really beautiful. I'll go and fetch it.' She returned with what the other describes as 'the ugliest, mangiest wig I'd ever seen'.

'Now put it on straightaway,' Jeritza insisted.

'Well, I must attend to some things first,' Nanette procrastinated.

Maria left but ten minutes later she was back. 'Why aren't you wearing the wig?' she demanded.

Nanette now had her excuse ready. 'Oh, your head is so much smaller than mine. I have a big head.'

Jeritza stalked out of the dressing-room and did not speak to her rival for months.

The Austrian was an expert scene-stealer. Long after her retirement, she attended a gala performance at the Met to mark the 50th anniversary of Martinelli's death. At the end all the celebrated singers present were lined up on the stage facing the audience. When invited to join them, Jeritza said with assumed modesty that she preferred to remain sitting where she was. The chairman of the Met made a speech and, after introducing to the audience all the stars on either side of him, he said, 'I think we also have Madame Jeritza in the house.' Whereupon she rose from her seat, flinging out her arms, and had the ovation of the evening.

Beverley Sill's singing teacher when the star was a small girl was Estelle Liebling, one of Jeritza's greatest friends, who had a penthouse in New York where the great prima donna and the hopeful pupil met and took to each other. Miss Sills says that her best moment came when she sang at a dinner party given by Jeritza. As a reward she gave the girl a gold toothpick and impressed upon her the need to rise out of her rut. 'You must become a character. You are too nice – too drab – no make-up. When the dinner is over, pick your teeth – then they will be talking about you.'

The friendship between the star and the beginner grew. Jeritza came to hear the girl sing in Haydn's *The Creation*, at which Beverley carried her score in a black leather folder like the other singers. Afterwards she received a note from Maria: 'Folder terrible. New one coming.' This turned out to be opulent and eye-catching, made of gold lamé encrusted with turquoises and other gems. 'How can I take that with me if I do the Verdi *Requiem*?' Beverley Sills recalls asking Jeritza. The reply came: 'I told you – you have to attract attention, lots of attention.'

★
The 'green' prima donna

★

Birgit Nilsson loves cooking as much she does singing. Her father, a farmer, sent her first to an agricultural school where she excelled at the culinary art. Years later, when she was a star at the Met, she would invite her friends to dine in her hotel suite, would cook and serve them Swedish dishes, then wash up herself.

As a singer, Miss Nilsson was largely self-taught, apart from some training at Stockholm's Royal School of Music. With her huge voice and passionate delivery, she was magnificent in Wagner's heroic roles. The range of her repertoire was impressive, leaving her without any rivals in the parts of Elektra, Leonora, Turandot, and Salome, thanks to her ability to alter the quality of her voice to suit the role. She learnt these on her own, without any coach, being an excellent musician, reading at sight and having instant recall.

When Birgit Nilsson sang Brünnhilde for the first time at Covent Garden Philip Hope-Wallace wrote: 'The voice is aquiline; it soars, swoops, wheels, pounces. It peals like an unsilenceable bell. It vies with the massed brass . . . It is like watching a show jumper. She cleared that fence with a lot to spare: how will she do it at the next water jump? Over! Gad, sir! That woman's a stunner. And so she is. Subtlety? Well, some Brünnhildes get more wisdom and pathos into it. But few in the audience cannot have thought themselves lucky, even blessed, to be present at this nightly display.'

The diva's favourite tenor was Wolfgang Windgassen who, singing Siegfried to her Brünnhilde in Florence, proved he was a perfect knight *sans peur et sans reproche*. When he found her asleep on a bed of rock and she awoke and rose, her costume came apart all the way down at the back. Clasping her in his arms, he gallantly fastened the hooks.

Not so easily put right was the problem at Birgit's Covent Garden début as Isolde, in April 1962. It was Friday the 13th.

Between the general rehearsal and the première, the colour of her costume was changed to a beautiful green, and next day, in a letter, she related her consequent unhappy experience. Putting on her new garment at the last minute, she discovered that it turned her 'green *all* over'. The overture began and she had to go on the stage as she was. Five minutes later, her hands were so green that she could not see the difference between them and her clothes. 'Brangane became green. Tristan almost all over green, and I was at the end of the act as green as a tree from top to bottom. Ah, boy! I have still no idea what I did on the stage.'

The second act went better because Birgit had time to change, but during the long love-duet she was stained green again through Tristan's remaining in the same rig. A postscript to her letter read: 'The man who spreaded my costume cried also. He had used water-colour instead of – I do not know what.'

★

Marguerite D'Alvarez, 'the most intellectual of palates'

★

The prima donna who enlivened her conversation with the most picturesque phrases was surely Marguerite D'Alvarez. Her accompanist for many years, Ivor Newton, found her a fascinating character. Of ample proportions, she had a queenly presence on the concert platform, with her classic features and creamy white complexion shown off to advantage by her black gown. There was a romantic aura about her which her eye-catching gems in antique settings helped to create: they looked, says Newton, 'as though they came from Lucrezia Borgia's jewel-case'.

'I have the blood of the Incas in my veins,' D'Alvarez liked to boast, and, giving full rein to her imagination, would go on to describe with graphic details her mother's wedding-dress 'woven by the Incas', her father's dinner-parties in the family's grandiose Peruvian home with a Chinese servant standing behind the chair of each one of the seventy guests, at which she was 'so happy that I danced my shoes to destruction'. In actual fact, D'Alvarez was born on Merseyside, where her father worked in the Peruvian consular service. When she told him she wanted to become a singer, he replied, according to her, that no Peruvian of their class would ever marry a singer. To which she retorted, 'Singing is more important than a husband.'

'I was born with an understanding of food and drink,' Newton heard her claim, 'and I have the most intellectual of palates.' Food inspired some of her most colourful metaphors. At a dinner, she told their hostess: 'What a delicious soufflé – it tastes like angels' saliva. I must send my photograph to your cook.' On another occasion, she exclaimed: 'This *vin rosé* has the colour of pounded rubies sparkling in the rays of the disappearing sun.' When presented with a bouquet of very full, white chrysanthemums, she remarked: 'How beautiful! They remind me of pregnant swans.'

Marguerite was certainly a gourmet: 'I don't go in for slimming,' she was reported as saying in the *Musical Times* of June 1932. 'My hips are part of my personality.'

★

Dame Kiri Te Kanawa

★

Dame Kiri Te Kanawa is one of the great operatic discoveries of our times, and became known to millions when she sang at the Royal Wedding in 1981. The many facets of her art, irresistible vivacity and sense of humour are brilliantly described by David Fingleton in his biography of her, one of the best of recent years, in which he also reveals an unexpected talent of Dame Kiri's for originating gourmet recipes. One of the first things she did on marriage was to buy a cordon-bleu course. Her friend, Veronica Haigh, has said that a meal prepared by the

Dame Kiri Te Kanawa, photographed by Christina Burton

singer, how ever simple, is invariably a gastronomic experience.

As a tribute to Dame Kiri, Anton Mosimann, the highly gifted Cuisinier of the Dorchester Hotel, has contributed to the collection of recipes given later in this book a new sweet which he calls *Crêpe sans Rival à la Kiri Te Kanawa*.

★

The prima donnas' favourite tipples

★

It may surprise many to learn that some divas of the last century very much liked drinking beer. The supreme soprano of her era, Milan-born Giulia Grisi who excelled both in coloratura and dramatic roles, preferred it to any other liquid refreshment, and it had no adverse effect on her figure for she still retained her slim beauty at forty. During the latter part of her career when she could not perform for long without tiring, a glass of porter would revive her. As Lucrezia Borgia in Donizetti's opera *Lucrezia*, she had to collapse on to the stage, and, lying there with her back to the audience, she would drink unseen a tankardful which had been passed up to her through a trapdoor.

According to impresario Alfred Bunn who presented her at Covent Garden and Drury Lane in the 1830s, Maria Malibran's favourite beverage was home-brewed beer, with which she ate onions. Before singing she often drank coffee with white burgundy or rum, sweetened with a great quantity of sugar – or a mysterious compound diluted with hot water, which she believed strengthened her voice. One day the Baron de Tréville called on Malibran and found her upset by a tale scandalmongers were spreading that she had become a dipsomaniac. This was because living at such high pressure during the day sometimes affected her balance, and this became noticeable when walking on the stage in the evenings. 'This is what I drink before singing!' Malibran cried, and seizing a china cup from the sideboard, she raised it to her visitor's lips and poured the

contents down his throat – much to his disgust, for they proved
to be a nauseous mixture of honey, barley-water and extract of
tar. 'That's unlikely to intoxicate anyone,' Malibran insisted,
'and yet they call me a drunkard.'

On another occasion, when she was due to leave home for the
opera-house, the diva went into the room where her husband
was finishing his meal and complained that a sore throat had
made her so hoarse that she could not sing a note and desperately needed some remedy for it. 'Ah! I see something that will
cure it!' she suddenly exclaimed and, seizing the pot of mustard
from the table, swallowed the whole of its contents.

On 26 May 1836, Malibran appeared in a new opera, *The
Maid of Artois*, at Covent Garden. During the rehearsals, much
to Alfred Bunn's annoyance, she absented herself to earn more
money by singing at morning concerts. This brought everything to a halt until she returned, and Bunn wrote in his
memoirs that the success of the production was put at risk by
'an unworthy grasp at a few pounds to the prejudice of a theatre
paying her nightly five times as much'. From the rise of the
curtain on the first night her performance bore the opera
triumphantly along, but when Bunn went into her dressing-
room during the interval before the last act, he saw that she was
exhausted. 'But,' said Malibran 'you angry devil, if you can
contrive to get me a pint of porter in the desert scene, you shall
have an encore to your finale.' Bunn was doubly involved in the
production's success, for as well as presenting *The Maid of
Artois* he had written the libretto to Balfe's music. He states,
'Had I been dealing with any other performer, I should perhaps
have hesitated in complying with a request that might have been
dangerous in its application at the moment; but to check her
powers was to annihilate them.' Therefore behind the hillock of
drifted sand on to which she sank towards the close of the scene,
he had an opening made in the floor of the stage through which a
pewter pot could be lifted up to Malibran's lips, while the
kneeling tenor, John Templeton, screened her from the audience's sight. 'The draught itself was so extremely refreshing,'
Bunn adds, 'that it was arranged during the subsequent run of

the opera for the negro slave at the head of the governor's procession to have in the gourd suspended to his neck the same quantity of the same beverage, to be applied to her lips on his first beholding the apparently dying Isolina.'

The Swedish Nightingale, Jenny Lind, was in the habit of taking a soup before she sang, as she found the combination of sago and eggs soothing to the chest and beneficial to the voice. Her recipe consisted of fine sago stewed in water, then mixed gradually with cream and egg-yolks, and finished with strong veal or beef stock.

Tetrazzini sustained herself during a performance by sipping sugared water out of a bottle between scenes. Birgit Nilsson at the Met drank orange juice with plenty of glucose dissolved in it, and after the final curtain she revived herself by taking a jigger of aquavit, a glass of beer, and a very special sort of herring, a supply of which she had brought over from her native Sweden. Joan Sutherland prefers blackcurrant syrup, and Eileen Farrell warm Coca-cola.

These liquids perform the very necessary service of keeping a vocalist's throat moist. But such necessities can become mere fads, as in the case of a certain tenor who was unable to sing without a special kind of lozenge in his mouth. Once he was about to embark on a difficult aria when the lozenge fell out, and he signalled desperately to his valet to pass him another one at once. But the box containing them had been left in the dressing-room and there was not enough time to fetch it. With admirable presence of mind, the valet tore a button off his jacket and creeping behind some scenic bushes succeeded in handing it surreptitiously. The tenor slipped it into his mouth without a glance, and, sucking happily away at the button, he sang gloriously. When he later discovered why the 'lozenge' had refused to dissolve, the shock freed him from his obsession, and he threw his remaining stock away.

★
Anna Pavlova

★

Let us leave the company of singing gourmets and turn to those who float through the air, light as soufflés. Sol Hurok, the American impresario who presented Pavlova in his country, never forgot the first time he ate in her company, in the outdoor restaurant at Palisades Park. He was so astonished that he just stared at her plate, ignoring what was on his own, for, he says, having sat at the same table as some famous singers he had become accustomed to large appetites, but never before had he dined with a dancer. In the years ahead he was to do so with many other ballerinas, and he found that they all ate like stevedores, devouring thick steaks, mountains of potatoes and quarts of milk. On consideration, he realized that in a single performance they must use up as much energy as any docker in a whole day's work, and needed to stoke up afterwards.

Touring in the States, Pavlova always ordered Russian food for her parties from New York. No matter how isolated or distant might be the place where she was dancing, a sucking pig had to be despatched to her in time for Easter, as well as pirozhki (pies filled with meat and rice, or fish, or cabbage stuffing), smoked salmon, and blinis with fresh caviar and sour cream.

Pavlova's husband, Victor Dandré, was very stout, and at table she used to stop him eating too much, therefore she could not understand why he still grew fatter. It was because once she was safely out of the way at the theatre, a waiter would stagger up to Victor's bedroom carrying a tray laden with rich food.

 # Coffee and liqueurs

★
Where stone angels sing
★

Nowhere has food been more happily married to music than in
Vienna. In 1786, when the city archives show the population to
have been less than a quarter of a million, they drank 473,339
casks of wine and 382,578 barrels of beer; and the animal
population bred for the table consisted of 42,197 oxen, 1,511
cows, 66,353 calves, 43,925 sheep, 164,700 lambs, 96,949 pigs,
and 12,967 sucking pigs. Dr Burney, visiting Vienna thirteen
years earlier, wrote that even the stone angels over the doors
sang. Music was an indispensable feature of every meal, with
the sounds of violin, flute, and zither forming a constant
background. Out at the palace of Schönbrunn, the chefs of Karl
Schwender's Coliseum group of restaurants and places of
amusement competed with one another to pander to the palates
of gourmets with delicacies that had such irresistible names as
Orpheus Sailing On A Grand Salmon, *Trout Minuet*, and *Fresco
of Boiled Salmon*. Those who could not afford such fine fare had
to content themselves with *schnitzel* or *backhändel*.

In 1717 Western Europe was saved from conquest by the
invading Turks when they were defeated at Belgrade by Prince

Eugène: the siege of Vienna was lifted, and the fleeing enemy abandoned outside the city walls a mountain of coffee in sacks. In London the sophisticated were already brewing it in small copper vessels over burning charcoal and drinking the thick, syrupy liquid thus produced. One Pasqua Rosée had opened the first public London coffee-house in St Michael's Alley in the middle of the previous century, claiming that the beverage 'quickens the spirits, and makes the heart lightsome' and 'yet is neither laxative, nor restringent'. His venture had not only succeeded but had been followed by a string of imitations. On the other side of the Channel, however, no similar interest had been shown until now.

An adventurous young man, Georg Kolschitzki, was the first to reach the Austrian capital with the news of the Turkish retreat, and he requested and received as his reward the coffee beans they had left behind. After roasting and grinding, he brewed them at home in a copper cauldron over a well-stoked fire, and obtained an intriguingly scented dark liquor which he sold from door to door. This so stimulated all who drank it that his sales soared. It was not long before, becoming more ambitious, he rented a room with a signboard outside bearing the words: '*Zur blauen Flasche*' ('At the blue bottle') and opened the first Viennese coffee-house. Here, thanks to a fortunate inspiration on his part, he served the elixir with either milk or cream. It proved such an instant success that others were soon copying him, and coffee-houses proliferated. In these, all classes gathered both to discuss business and for relaxation, and – the Viennese being music-lovers – an essential added attraction was an orchestra of appropriate size.

With the coffee, it was soon the custom to serve whipped cream, *schlagobers*. While enjoying this, and pastries, the customers would discuss the latest gossip and search the columns of the newspapers for appetizing titbits, such as the lengthy correspondence in 1877 between Richard Wagner and a milliner. Letters were shown to that coffee-lover, Brahms (whose stepmother, by the way, was a cook), who was amused to find that the musician he so disliked was as anxious as any high-society woman that his dressing-gowns should match the colours of the furnishings in his bedroom and study. To Fräulein Berthe, he had written, 'You are well acquainted with the model I need for my house robes. Can you get me some dark pink satin? Can the enclosed shade for light pink be bought for 4 or 5 florins? Have you any of the dark yellow material left from which we made the drapes for the little table?' In another letter, Wagner told the lady, 'Unfortunately, I cannot send you any money this week as my affairs are not going well. Do not worry though. I most urgently want to reimburse you as soon as possible.' And a short while later, he had written to the milliner, 'Please see my enclosed sketch. Now how much will such a dressing gown cost? . . .'

Brahms passed the correspondence on to a journalist, Daniel Spilzer, who arranged for the *Neue Frei Presse* of Vienna to buy and print them, and for days they were talked about in the coffee-houses.

★
Bach's 'Coffee Cantata'
★

In 1707 Johann Sebastian Bach, at the start of his musical career, was employed as town organist in Mulhausen, for which he received an annual salary of 85 gulden (£10.60) together with fifty-four bushels of grain, three lbs of fish, and eight trusses of faggots and wood for kindling. Twenty-two years later, he was appointed head of the Collegium Musicum of Leipzig, an association of young musicians who gained experience by meeting every week to play together in public. Later, on summer Wednesdays between 4 and 6 p.m. they gave open-air concerts at Zimmermann's coffee-house on the outskirts of the city.

This experience inspired Bach to compose his nearest attempt at an operatic work, Opus 211, the 'Coffee Cantata' for three singers, strings and flute. It is really a sort of humorous oratorio, with verses by Picander telling how the soprano, Liesgen, has become addicted to a new beverage popular with young people: coffee. Her father, Schendrian, described as 'an old stick-in-the-mud', tries in vain to make her give up drinking what he loathes by threatening to confiscate her modish crinoline. But she yields it only when he promises, as a *quid pro quo*, to find her a fine husband, and father hurries off in search of one. Picander's text ends here, but Bach adds some amusing further twists to the plot. In a recitative, Liesgen reveals her intention to insist on a clause in the marriage-contract giving her the right to drink coffee whenever she wishes. Her parent concedes defeat, and the cantata concludes with a recitative in which the trio agree that the coffee craze has come to stay.

★

Huysmans' extraordinary 'mouth organ'

★

J. K. Huysmans has been described as the 'First Decadent' by James Laver, who also said that 'all the prose works of the Decadence from Lorrain to Gourmont, Wilde and D'Annunzio are contained in embryo in *A Rebours*'. The main character of Huysmans' celebrated novel is Des Esseintes, and the furnishing of his house at Fontenoy occupies a large part of the book. Modelled upon a real person, Count Robert de Montesquiou, Des Esseintes, longing for alcoholic stimulation, visits the dining-room and slides back a secret panel revealing his 'Mouth Organ', as he jestingly calls the small barrels resting side by side on sandalwood bars, each with a silver tap, labelled 'Flute, 'Horn', 'Voix Celeste', and so on, and with tiny cups ready below.

According to Des Esseintes, each liqueur corresponds in taste to the sound of a musical instrument. Dry curaçao, for instance, resembles the smooth sharpness of the clarinet; kümmel the sonorous yet nasal oboe; crême-de-menthe and anisette the flute, at the same time sweet and peppery, soft and yet wailing; kirsch is like a fierce trumpet; gin and whisky attack the palate like strident cornets and trombones; brandy conjures up the overwhelming crash of tubas; and raki from Chios is like the clang of cymbals and the thunder of drums.

Des Esseintes believes that one might be able to play string quartets on the palate, with the violin impersonated by a rare cognac, the viola by rum, the cello by vespetro, and the double-bass by fine old bitters. One might even make the performance a quintet by adding yet another instrument – the harp, for which one would need a few drops of dry cumin.

In the novel, Des Esseintes finds it possible to execute on his tongue a succession of voiceless melodies and to 'hear' in his mouth solos of crême-de-menthe and duets of vespetro and rum. He even succeeds in transferring to his palate selections of real music, following the composer's motif step by step, expressing his thoughts and echoing every nuance of effect by mixing now kindred, now disparate, liqueurs.

Becoming more ambitious, Des Esseintes composes pieces of his own such as pastoral symphonies, reproducing in his throat the song of the nightingale by tasting cassis, and syrupy, sentimental airs with the aid of crême-de-cacao. Huysmans ends Des Esseintes' flight of fancy by declaring that on this particular evening he is not in the mood for music so he drinks instead a glass of Irish whiskey.

Emile Zola, describing a food-market in his novel *The Fat and Thin*, found that the bouquet of the cheeses made him hear orchestral music. He wrote: 'The Cantal, the Cheshire, and the goats' milk cheese seemed to be snoring out deep breaths like the prolonged tones of a bassoon, amidst which could be recognized, like detached notes, the sharp whiffs of the Neufchâtels, the Troyes, and the Mont d'Or.'

Harold Acton, staying in Shanghai in the early 1930s, advanced in his *Memoirs of an Aesthete* the theory that meat is the Western substitute for sound above a certain pitch. 'The meat we assimilate replaces the clash of gongs and tintinnabulation of cymbals, hence physically we can bear no more, our ears contract in misery at a Chinese theatre.' He continues that the Chinese, being less carnivorous than Westerners, enjoy what they call *jê-nao*, of which 'hot din' is a literal translation. This is an essential accompaniment to aimless amusement, and a spicy odour characteristic of a race nurtured on rice. After living for several years on Chinese food, Acton's own attitude changed, and the loud gongs, cymbals, and *hu-ch'in* became 'sweetly soothing' to his nerves. He had only to listen to them to recover his serenity on a sultry day, whereas a Western band affected him 'like a dirge'.

This interrelation between the senses of taste and sound inspired Sir Thomas Beecham to call 'lollipops' the pieces of music played as encores at the end of his concerts, when – as he put it – his audience declined to depart 'until, emulating Oliver Twist, it has obtained an extra helping'.

As his programmes usually concluded with 'a grand bang or explosion of sound', Beecham's practice was to play an encore which was in complete contrast. He explained: 'The piece selected has generally been of an essentially syrupy, soapy, soothing, and even soporific nature, and the effect upon the audience has been that its emotional temperature, raised to a high point at the conclusion of the actual programme, is gradually reduced to the normal, so that everyone walks out happy and comfortable.' The same effect, in fact, as a piece of candy on a stick has on a child.

Reflections upon paying

★

The greatest of sacrifices

★

Renouncing the pleasures of gourmet cooking is for some the greatest of sacrifices. For five years before her notable début at the Met in 1949, the soprano Astrid Várnay spent all her spare time either cooking or studying educational books. Operatic success led to so many singing engagements that she had to give up the latter, but an irresistible interest in new recipes kept her in the kitchen whenever at home. One evening, as she lay dying as Brünnhilde on the stage at Covent Garden, Astrid decided that it was foolish to go on pandering to her appetite at the expense of her mind, so she renounced cooking and restricted her eating. 'They are both terrific time-wasters,' she was reported as saying in *Opera News* of January 1954. 'Now I pack my own lunch and take it to the Met, then during the break I eat it in the electricians' room where I can read about lighting and make-up. It's a very sparse lunch – sometimes just a lettuce and tomato salad, and an apple.'

Thackeray would not have approved. He once wrote to a friend: 'Sir, respect your dinner, idolize it, enjoy it properly. You will be by many hours in the week, many weeks in the year, and many years in your life, happier if you do. Don't tell me it is not worthy of a man. All man's senses are worthy of employment, and should be cultivated as a duty . . . remember that every man who has been worth a fig in this world as poet, painter, or musician, has had a good appetite, and a good taste.'

PART
II

 Author's list of recipes

The author has collected well over one hundred rare recipes, the brain-children of great chefs who have ministered to the palates of composers, singers, and musicians, and who named them after favourite clients or their celebrated operas. An alphabetical list of these dishes follows, with asterisks against certain of them, some elaborate and others simple, for which the recipes are given subsequently. This may sufficiently whet the appetites of those interested in cooking for them to try their hands at making these delicacies. To aid those embarking on such gastronomic adventures, separate instructions are given for preparing the classic sauces required in some cases.

Aida, Bombe
Aida, Salade

Belle Hélène, Poires
Belle Hélène, Salade
Bellini, Fiori di latte à la
Bellini, Ravioles à la
Bizet, Consommé
Bizet, Oeufs
Boieldieu, Oeufs pochés à la
Brillat-Savarin, Bordure de pommes

Brillat-Savarin, Boston fondue à la
Brillat-Savarin, Consommé
*Brillat-Savarin, Flan
Brillat-Savarin, Perdreau en crépine
Brillat-Savarin, Poires

Calvé, Coupe Emma
Carmen, Consommé
Carmen, Glace
Carmen, Oeufs
Carmen, Salade
*Caruso, Spaghetti à la
Chaliapin, Bortsch

Delmonico, Oeufs
Delmonico, Potatoes style Lorenzo
Diva, Soufflé de Saumon
Don Giovanni, Cream puffs

*Figaro, Cold lobster
Figaro, Tournedos
Fra Diavolo, Homard

Garden, Coupe Mary
*Garden, Poires Mary
Gounod, Purée of pea soup

Halevy, Oeufs

*Kanawa, Crêpe sans rival à la Kiri Te

Manon, Gâteau
*Manon, Oeufs pochés
Manon, Pike à la
Manon, Yeast cake
Massenet, Garnish
Massenet, Oeufs brouillés
Massenet, Oeufs pochés
Melba, Coupe
Melba, Noisette d'agneau

*Melba, Pêches
Melba, Poires
Melba, Sauce
Meyerbeer, Oeufs au miroir à la
Meyerbeer, Mignons de filet à la
Mignon, Oeufs

*Nordica, Chicken

*Offenbach, Oeufs Jacques
Opéra, Cassolette
Opéra, Charlotte
Opéra, Crême Moulée
Opéra, Oeufs
Otello, Chicken
*Otello, Salade
*Otero, Filets de sole

Paganini, Selle d'agneau à la
Patti, Chocolate kisses à la Adelina
Patti, Coupe Adelina
Patti, Oeufs pochés
Patti, Potage de légumes Adelina
*Patti, Poularde Adelina
Puccini, Small fowl Giacomo

Rector, Eggs à la
Rector-style:
   Crabmeat Mornay
   Filet mignon Hederer
   *Sole Marguéry
*Rigoletto, Cream of green pea soup
Rigoletto, Oeufs
Rossini, Coquilles de volaille
*Rossini, Côtelettes d'agneau
Rossini, Escalopes de Foie Gras
Rossini, Escalopes de ris de veau
Rossini, Garniture
Rossini, Oeufs brouillés
Rossini, Oeufs pochés

Rossini, Oeufs sur le plat
Rossini, Omelette
*Rossini, Poularde à la
Rossini, Suprême de caneton
Rossini, Suprême de perdreau
Rossini, Suprême de volaille
Rossini, Tournedos

Semiramis, Mousse à la
Strauss, Gâteau Johann
*Strauss, Wiener schnitzel Johann

Tetrazzini, Chicken
Tetrazzini, Lobster
*Tetrazzini, Tuna
Thaïs, Coupe
Tosca, Amourette
Tosca, Barquette
Tosca, Bombe
Tosca, Cream of broccoli
Tosca, Fraises
Tosca, Poularde
*Tosca, Salade
Tosca, Turbot
Traviata, Bombe

*Verdi, Sole
Verdi, Suprême de Poulet

 # Recipes in full

Soup

CREAM OF GREEN PEA SOUP RIGOLETTO
(a Viennese recipe)

1 lb (450 g) fresh green peas	2 lettuce leaves
1 oz (25 g) butter	1 sprig parsley
1 oz (25 g) cornflour	½ cup single cream
1½ cups of chicken stock	1 egg yolk
1 onion	¼ cup chopped spinach leaves

Prepare a purée of the cooked peas, reserving some of the cooking liquid. In another pan, melt the butter and blend in the cornflour, cooking slowly and stirring constantly until it turns golden. Add a little of the liquid in which the peas were cooked, and the chicken stock, still stirring. Add the finely sliced onion, lettuce leaves, and parsley. Season, and simmer for 15 mins. Add the pea purée and blend in well. Beat the egg yolk with the cream and stir into the soup gradually: allow to heat, but not to boil. Simmer with the chopped spinach leaves for 10 mins.

This soup should be served with toast which has been coated with cheese-soufflé mixture, dusted with Parmesan cheese, and then oven-baked until it is puffed and golden.

Eggs

OEUFS JACQUES OFFENBACH

6 eggs
3 oz (75 g) tuna fish
6 large shrimps
½ teaspoon finely chopped
parsley

6 pieces of toast spread with
butter and tomato paste,
lightly grilled
12 anchovy fillets (or strips of
pimento)

Beat the eggs lightly with a fork, then add the tuna fish flaked into fine pieces. Chop the shrimps well, and add them with the parsley to the mixture. Cook it very slowly in a saucepan, until the eggs reach the consistency of a custard. Serve on the prepared toast, and garnish each with 2 anchovy fillets or the strips of pimento.

OEUFS POCHÉS MANON

2 tablespoons chopped onion
1 chopped leek (white part
only)
2 tablespoons olive oil
1 dessertspoon curry powder
2 tomatoes
⅓ clove of garlic
1 bouquet garni

1 teaspoon salt
4 crushed peppercorns
1 lb (450 g) whitebait
A few leaves of saffron
6 poached eggs
6 croûtons

Brown the onion and leek in the hot olive oil. Add the curry powder, the sliced and skinned tomatoes, the crushed garlic and the bouquet garni. Cover and sauté for about 10 mins, then add 1¾ pts (1 litre) of boiling water, together with salt and crushed peppercorns. Boil for about 3 mins, and then add whitebait and saffron. Continue boiling for about 12 mins more. Rub all through a sieve into a clean saucepan and keep hot.

Arrange the 6 poached eggs on the same number of croûtons (bread fried in oil) in a deep serving dish. Pour over this the liquor.

Pasta

SPAGHETTI À LA CARUSO
(recipe by Louis Diat)

For 1 lb (450 g) spaghetti:

2 finely chopped onions	¼ lb (100 g) chicken livers
1 tablespoon butter	1 teaspoon parsley
6 tomatoes	1 small clove of garlic,
½ pt (300 ml) beef gravy	chopped
6 or 8 sliced mushrooms	6 oz (150 g) grated Parmesan
4 or 6 diced artichoke hearts	cheese

Peel, chop finely, and cook the tomatoes. Brown the onions in a saucepan with the butter, then add tomatoes and gravy. Sauté the mushrooms, artichoke hearts, and the chicken livers in olive oil, stir them into the contents of the saucepan, and add the chopped parsley and the well-crushed clove of garlic. Season. Cook the spaghetti in boiling salted water for about 15 minutes: drain, and place in hot serving dish. Sprinkle with the grated Parmesan cheese, and pour over it the prepared sauce. Serve very hot, with extra grated Parmesan to be added by the diners according to taste.

Pastry

FLAN BRILLAT-SAVARIN

6 oz (150 g) sifted plain flour
3 oz (75 g) butter
2 egg yolks
2 fl oz (50 ml) water
½ teaspoon salt

Eggs scrambled with cream
Truffles
Butter
Grated Parmesan cheese

Put the flour on a board, make a well in the centre, and place in it the next 4 ingredients. Work them in the well with the finger-tips, and when blended mix in the flour a little at a time. Once this is done, clean the fingers, then smooth the paste out with the heel of the hand, stopping once the paste binds together. Roll into a ball, wrap in a cloth, or greaseproof paper, and chill for at least 2 hours. Then line a flan tin, and bake it 'blind'.

Fill the cooked flan case with a mixture of the scrambled eggs and truffles. Season a few strips of truffle, dip them in melted butter, and use to decorate. Sprinkle with grated Parmesan, pour over the remaining melted butter, and brown in a hot oven.

Fish and Shellfish

COLD LOBSTER FIGARO

2 live lobsters, weighing
  about 1½ lb (600 g) each
Court bouillon or vegetable
  stock
1 teaspoon each of chopped
  chives, chervil and
  tarragon

½ teaspoon of cayenne
1 tablespoon of mayonnaise
Strips of pimento
Anchovy fillets
Capers
Aspic jelly

Boil the lobsters in the bouillon or stock, and allow to cool in the liquor, then remove and drain well. Lay them on a chopping board, back uppermost, and with a strong knife split them in two lengthwise. Remove the bag from the heads and reserve the green creamy livers. Take out the tail-meat in one piece, and trim lightly. Crack the claws and finely chop their meat: to it add the tail trimmings, the liver, and the chopped herbs, and bind with the mayonnaise to which has been added the cayenne. Fill the half-shells with this, replace on top the whole pieces of tail-meat, and decorate with thin strips of pimento, anchovy fillets and capers. Coat the whole with aspic jelly and serve with mayonnaise or Sauce Verte (see page 224).

SOLE MARGUÉRY RECTOR-STYLE

This is the method used by George Rector to prepare this dish in his restaurant, as given by him in his reminiscences. He used Dover soles imported from England, and cut 4 fillets from each fish. He then boiled the bones and trimmings for 8–12 hours, with plenty of leeks, carrots, turnips, lettuce, and parsley, until it was reduced to a concentrated jelly.

In the top of a double-boiler he mixed the yolks of 4 dozen eggs with a gallon of melted butter, which he stirred over hot water in the base of the double-boiler as one would do for hollandaise sauce. He added every 10 mins a pint of dry white wine, and also from time to time a spoonful of the fish fumet, finishing it with a dash of cayenne and salt. At no time was the sauce allowed to boil. Then it was strained through a very fine sieve.

Once the sauce was ready, the sole fillets were taken from the ice and placed in a pan with about ½″ of water, just enough to float them a little. After the water had boiled for 10–15 mins, he removed them and placed them on a silver platter garnished at one end with small shrimps and at the other end with mussels imported from Northern France. The sauce was poured liberally over the sole, sprinkled with chopped parsley, and placed under a hot grill until it was all golden-brown.

FILETS DE SOLE OTERO
(recipe from Maxim's in its early days)

1½ lb (600 g) filleted Dover
   or lemon sole
1 wineglass of white wine
1 chopped onion
1 sprig of thyme
½ bayleaf
Grated cheese

Finely chopped parsley
Few drops of lemon juice
One large potato for each
   diner
1 tablespoon shrimps
2 egg yolks
5 oz (125 g) melted butter

Prepare a fish fumet from the bones and trimmings of the sole, together with the wine, onion, thyme, bayleaf, parsley and lemon juice. Poach the skinned fillets of sole in this. Bake some large potatoes and scoop out the insides, taking great care to keep the shells whole.

Prepare a white wine sauce by boiling down ¼ pt (150 ml) of the fish fumet by about two-thirds. Cool slightly, add the egg yolks and whisk over a low heat until it thickens. Add the melted butter a little at a time, beating continually. Season and strain the sauce through a cloth or fine sieve. Add to it the shrimps, and garnish the bottoms of the potato shells with this. Place a poached fillet on this, in each shell, then cover with enough Sauce Mornay (see page 223) to fill the shells. Sprinkle with grated cheese, reheat in the oven, and serve very hot.

TUNA TETRAZZINI

6 oz (150 g) spaghetti
3 tablespoons chopped onion
1 tablespoon olive oil
1 tin (10.6 oz, 300 g) of
   mushroom soup
¼ cup grated Parmesan

1 cup flaked tuna fish
⅓ cup olives
1 tablespoon chopped parsley
1 teaspoon lemon juice
A pinch of dried thyme and
   marjoram

Cook the spaghetti and keep warm. Sauté the chopped onion in the olive oil, then add the mushroom soup, diluted with ½ cup of water, and ⅛ cup of the grated Parmesan cheese. Stir in the flaked tuna fish (shrimps may be used as an alternative) and the pitted and sliced olives. Heat well. Add the parsley, lemon juice, and herbs. Mix all with the drained spaghetti, place in a buttered casserole dish, and sprinkle with the rest of the cheese. Heat under the grill until lightly browned.

SOLE VERDI

½ lb (200 g) macaroni
½ pt (300 ml) double cream
¼ cup grated Gruyère
¼ cup grated Parmesan
3 oz (75 g) cooked, flaked lobster meat

¾ lb (300 g) cooked mushrooms
4 sole fillets
½ cup white wine
1 cup Sauce Mornay (see page 223)

Cook the macaroni in boiling water until tender, and drain. Mix with the cream. Fork in lightly the two grated cheeses and add the lobster. Fold in the finely chopped, cooked mushrooms. Poach the fillets of sole in the white wine diluted with a little water. Transfer the macaroni and lobster mixture to a serving dish, spreading it out evenly, and place the cooked fillets on it, salting them to taste. Coat with the Sauce Mornay.

Meat

CÔTELETTES D'AGNEAU ROSSINI
(recipe from the Maison D'Or, Paris)

Fry some lamb chops in butter, and arrange them on a dish. Top each with a slice of foie gras lightly fried in butter, and with two or three slivers of truffle tossed in butter. Dilute the pan juices with a little Madeira (or any similar wine); add to this some Demi-glace Sauce (see page 222); boil down; strain and pour over the chops.

WIENER SCHNITZEL JOHANN STRAUSS

4 veal escalopes about 6 oz (150 g) each	1 lemon
	4 stoned olives
Flour	4 anchovy fillets
1 egg	Chopped parsley
White breadcrumbs	Anchovy butter
3 oz (75 g) butter	

Pound thin the escalopes, dip them in lightly seasoned flour, shake them, and brush them with egg beaten with salt and a few drops of olive oil. Melt the butter in a frying-pan, lay the escalopes in it and fry, turning once, until they are golden-brown and tender to a fork. Cover with breadcrumbs, and place on a hot flat dish, on a thin layer of anchovy butter, made by de-salting and drying anchovy fillets, and pounding them in a mortar with just over twice their weight of butter, then rubbing them through a fine sieve. Garnish each escalope with a slice of peeled lemon and a stoned olive surrounded by an anchovy fillet. Squeeze a little lemon juice over the melted butter left in the pan, and strain over the dish. Sprinkle with the parsley and serve at once.

Poultry

CHICKEN NORDICA
(Created for Lillian Nordica by a New York chef)

A 4-lb (1800 g) roasting chicken	½ cup chopped parsley
	4 eggs
1 large onion	¼ cup soft breadcrumbs
3 oz (75 g) butter	½ cup Madeira or sherry
½ lb (200 g) chopped chicken liver	2 tablespoons butter
	2 thin slices ham
¼ lb (100 g) finely minced veal	Salt and pepper

Sauté the chopped onion in the melted 3 oz butter; add the liver, veal, parsley and season to taste. Cook for 5 mins, stirring all the time over a low heat. Then bind together with the beaten yolks of the 4 eggs, and the breadcrumbs, and stuff the chicken with this mixture. Place one slice of ham on each side of the chicken, and roast in a slow oven, basting occasionally with the 2 tablespoons of butter melted in the Madeira or sherry.

POULARDE ADELINA PATTI
(recipe by Escoffier)

A 4-lb (1800 g) roasting
   chicken
1 oz (25 g) butter
3 oz (75 g) rice
½ pt (300 ml) stock
2 oz (50 g) truffles

2 oz (50 g) foie gras
2 tablespoons meat jelly
2 slices fat bacon
1½ pts (900 ml) Sauce
   Suprême (see page 223)

Prepare the stuffing by cooking the rice for a few minutes in half the butter, in a saucepan, and then adding the stock and cooking for 20 mins more. Remove from the heat, add the chopped truffles, the foie gras and meat jelly, and mix all thoroughly. Season the chicken, stuff it with the mixture, and truss it with legs folded back. Cover the breast with bacon, and brush all over with the rest of the melted butter. Cook for about an hour in a moderate oven.

Make the Sauce Suprême, adding a little paprika.

Place cooked chicken on a serving dish, untrussed; surround it with slices of foie gras, and coat with a little of the sauce. Garnish with freshly cooked globe artichoke hearts decorated with buttered asparagus tips and julienne strips of truffle. Serve the rest of the Sauce Suprême separately.

POULARDE À LA ROSSINI
(recipe by Escoffier)

A 3-lb (1500 g) roasting
  chicken
4 oz (100 g) foie gras
4 oz (100 g) chopped truffles

1 slice fat bacon
2 oz (50 g) butter
½ pint (300 ml) brown veal
  stock

Season the inside of the chicken with salt and pepper, and stuff
with the foie gras and the truffles. Truss it, cover the breast with
the bacon, and roast gently in the butter, basting frequently.
Pour off excess butter from pan, add the brown veal stock and
stir well. Bring to boil, and reduce heat slightly. Put a little of
the sauce on a serving dish and place the chicken on top. Serve
the remaining sauce separately, and with a dish of buttered
noodles, grated cheese and mashed pâté de foie gras.

Salads

SALADE OTELLO
(recipe by Louis Diat of the Ritz-Carlton)

Dice equal amounts of pineapple and boiled potatoes, and add
to them the same quantities of a julienne of ham and celery. Mix
all with a light mayonnaise, to ¼ pt (150 ml) of which has been
added 1 tablespoon of whipped cream and the juice of half a
lemon.

SALADE TOSCA
(recipe by Escoffier)

4 cooked chicken breasts
4 slices white truffles
1 head of celery

4 oz (100 g) Parmesan cheese
4 hard-boiled egg yolks
Chopped parsley and
  tarragon

Cut the chicken, truffles and celery into small pieces and mix well. Prepare a dressing of 3 parts olive oil to 1 part wine vinegar, with ½ teaspoon each of salt and freshly ground black pepper, and a little anchovy essence. Pour over the mixture, and sprinkle with the grated Parmesan cheese, sieved hard-boiled egg yolks, chopped parsley and tarragon.

Dessert

PÊCHES MELBA
(recipe by Escoffier)

4–6 ripe peaches, according to size	4 oz (100 g) icing-sugar
1 pt (600 ml) vanilla ice-cream	1 lemon
	1 lb (450 g) raspberries, fresh or frozen

Peel the peaches, rub them with a cut lemon and sprinkle with sugar to prevent browning. Cover with cling-film and chill. Rub the raspberries through a sieve and gradually add the icing-sugar to sweeten well. Chill both this purée and the coupe glasses. Just before serving, put the vanilla ice-cream into the bottom of each coupe, top with a peach (whole or halved, according to size), and spoon some purée over the peach. Serve at once.

POIRES MARY GARDEN
(recipe by Escoffier)

Pears	Glacé cherries
Light sugar syrup	Whipped cream
Raspberry sauce (see page 222)	

Cut in half some fine pears, removing pips and cores. Peel and place at once in the light sugar syrup, poaching them slowly until they are tender but not soft. Cool them, and place them in a large, flat, dessert dish. Cover them with the raspberry sauce to which chopped glacé cherries have been added, and decorate with the whipped cream forced through an icing nozzle. (Sauce and whipped cream must be added just before serving.)

CRÊPE SANS RIVAL À LA KIRI TE KANAWA
(a new, unpublished recipe by Anton Mosimann,
Cuisinier at the Dorchester Hotel, London)

The pancakes:

6 tablespoons (100 ml) milk	½ oz (15 g) sugar
2 oz (60 g) flour	Scant ½ oz (10 g) melted
1 egg yolk	butter
1 whole egg	Butter for frying pancakes

Put the milk and flour into a bowl and mix well. Add the egg yolk, the whole egg, and the sugar, and mix well. Add the melted butter and pass the mixture through a sieve. Fry the pancakes, very thin.

The filling:

⅓ pt (200 ml) vanilla cream (see below)	1 dessertspoon (10 ml) Pernod
½ pt (300 ml) hazelnuts, finely ground	5 oz (125 g) cranberries, boiled in 1 oz (25 g) sugar
Scant 2 oz (40 g) marzipan	4 Kiwi fruits

Mix the vanilla cream with the finely ground hazelnuts, marzipan, and cranberries, and finish with the Pernod. Spread the pancakes thinly with this mixture, and lay some finely sliced Kiwi fruits down the centre of each pancake. Fold the pancakes over from both sides.

The garnish:

¼ pt (150 ml) meringue
   italienne (see below)
1 oz (25 g) finely ground
   hazelnuts

⅓ pt (200 ml) raspberry sauce
   (see next page)
A few cranberries

Garnish with the meringue italienne to which the ounce of ground hazelnuts has been added. Bake the pancakes in a warm oven for 4–5 mins, then pour some raspberry sauce on a plate and place the pancakes on it. Decorate with a few cranberries and serve immediately. The special point about this sweet is that the pancakes should be served hot while the filling is cold.

VANILLA CREAM (CRÈME PATISSIERE)

Scant ½ pt (250 ml) milk
½ vanilla pod
3 egg yolks

3¼ oz (80 g) sugar
1½ oz (40 g) flour

Bring the milk to the boil with the vanilla pod in a saucepan. Mix the egg yolks, sugar and flour together in a bowl. Add the boiling milk and mix in well. Return the mixture to the saucepan and bring slowly to the boil. Continue to boil for 2 to 3 mins, stirring constantly. Strain through a fine sieve.

MERINGUE ITALIENNE

4 oz (100 g) sugar
2 fl oz (50 ml) water

2 egg whites
¾ oz (20 g) icing sugar

Place and heat the sugar and water in a heavy pan and stir until sugar is dissolved. Cook until the syrup reaches 100–115°C (210–240°F). Meanwhile, beat the egg whites until stiff and fold in the icing sugar. Add the cooked syrup slowly (in threads) to the beaten egg whites, and continue beating till the mixture is cool.

RASPBERRY SAUCE

9 oz (250 g) ripe raspberries
3¼ oz (80 g) caster sugar

juice of 1 lemon
a little Himbeergeist
(raspberry liqueur)

Purée the raspberries. Add the caster sugar. Flavour with the lemon juice and Himbeergeist. Strain the mixture through a fine sieve to remove the pips.

Note: to ensure that this sauce has a fresh taste, it is very important to use only the freshest and ripest raspberries.

Sauces

SAUCE DEMI-GLACE

1¼ pts (750 ml) brown stock
1 onion
1 carrot
2 tablespoons flour
1 bouquet garni
2 tablespoons tomato purée

2 mushrooms
1 clove
6 black peppercorns
2 oz (50 g) butter
1 oz (25 g) lean ham or bacon
½ gill (75 ml) sherry

Melt the butter in a pan and add the ham cut into small pieces. Fry for a few minutes then add the sliced vegetables, the herbs and spices. Stir over a low heat for about 5 mins, then add the flour and brown it carefully. Add the stock, tomato purée, and sherry, and stir until boiling, then lower the heat and let it simmer for at least 30 mins, stirring occasionally. Skim off the fat and strain through a fine sieve.

For Sauce Demi-glace, boil ½ pt (300 ml) of this basic Sauce Espagnole until well reduced, and then add ¼ pt (150 ml) of good gravy; season to taste with salt and pepper, simmer for about 10 mins, then use.

SAUCE MORNAY

1½ oz (40 g) flour	1 bouquet garni
2 oz (50 g) butter	10 peppercorns, white
1 small onion	½ bayleaf
1¼ pts (750 ml) hot milk	1 blade of mace
2 tablespoons finely chopped ham	Seasoning of grated nutmeg, cayenne and salt

Make a basic Sauce Béchamel by bringing the milk to the boil with the onion, bouquet garni, peppercorns, mace and bayleaf. In another saucepan melt the butter, stir in the flour, and cook a little without browning. Stir in the milk mixture gradually; whisk until it boils: add the chopped ham; then simmer for about 50 mins stirring occasionally, until it is reduced to about two-thirds of the original quantity. Strain through a fine sieve, pressing the ham, etc, to extract all the liquid. Return to pan and season lightly with a pinch each of cayenne and grated nutmeg, and ½ teaspoon salt.

To convert this Sauce Béchamel into Sauce Mornay, blend it with some of the stock or fumet in which the fish was cooked, then stir in a mixture of 1 oz each of grated Gruyère and Parmesan cheeses, and ½ teaspoon English or French mustard. Reheat but do not boil. (The sauce can be further enriched by adding an egg yolk blended with a little cream.)

SAUCE SUPRÊME

A scant pt (500 ml) chicken stock
½ pt (300 ml) fresh cream
2 oz (50 g) unsalted butter

Boil the chicken stock in a saucepan until it is reduced to half its original quantity, adding the cream meanwhile. When it will coat the back of a spoon, remove from the heat and stir in the butter. Strain and keep hot till required.

SAUCE VERTE

½ pt (300 ml) mayonnaise
1 dessertspoon lemon juice
1 oz (25 g) spinach leaves

1 oz (25 g) watercress leaves
1 oz (25 g) finely chopped
    chervil, parsley and
    tarragon

Blanch the spinach and watercress for a couple of minutes in boiling water, refresh under a cold tap in a colander, wrap in a clean fine cloth and squeeze the green juice through into a jug (or else pound the leaves in a mortar and press through a sieve). Add slowly to the mayonnaise, whisking all the time. Beat in the finely chopped herbs. Add the lemon juice, then pepper and salt to taste. Chill for a few hours so that the flavours can develop.

 Selected Bibliography

ACTON, HAROLD, *Memoirs of an Aesthete*, Methuen, London, 1948

ADLON, HEDDA, *Hotel Adlon*, Barrie Books, London, 1958

ALDA, FRANCES, *Men, Women and Tears*, Houghton Mifflin, Boston, 1937

AMORY, CLEVELAND, *The Proper Bostonians*, E. P. Dutton, New York, 1955

ANDRIEU, PIERRE, *Fine bouche. A history of the restaurant in France*, Cassell, London, 1958

ARESTY, ESTHER BRADFORD, *The delectable past. The joys of the table*, Allen & Unwin, London, 1965

BALDICK, ROBERT, *The First Bohemian. The life of Henri Murger*, Hamish Hamilton, London, 1961

BARBAUD, PIERRE, *Haydn*, John Calder, London, 1959

BARZUN, JACQUES, *Pleasures of Music*, Michael Joseph, London, 1952

BAYARD, JEAN EMILE, *Montmartre, Past and Present*, T. Fisher Unwin, London, 1926

BEEBE, LUCIUS, *The Big Spenders*, Hutchinson, London, 1967

BEER, THOMAS, *The Mauve Decade*, Random House, New York, 1961

BEETON, ISABELLA MARY, *The Book of Household Management*, S. O. Beeton, London, 1861

BERLIOZ, LOUIS HECTOR, *Life and Letters*, Remington & Co, London, 1882

BEYLE, M. H., *Life of Rossini*, John Calder, London, 1956

BOULESTIN, XAVIER MARCEL, *Myself. My Two Centuries*, Cassell, London, 1936

– *Ease and Endurance*, Home & Van Thal, London, 1945

– *The Best of Boulestin*, Heinemann, London, 1952

BOWDEN, GREGORY HOUSTON, *British Gastronomy: the Rise of Great Restaurants*, Chatto & Windus, London, 1975

BROUGH, JAMES, *Miss Lillian Russell*, McGraw Hill, New York, 1978

BROWN, H. C. *Brownstone Fronts and Saratoga Trunks*, E. P. Dutton, New York, 1935

– *Fifth Avenue*, Fifth Avenue Association, New York, 1924

– *The Story of Old New York*, E. P. Dutton, New York, 1934

CALVÉ, EMMA, *My Life*, D. Appleton & Co, New York, 1922

CANTOR, EDWARD, and FREEDMAN, DAVID, *Ziegfeld, the Great Glorifier*, A. H. King, New York, 1934

CARTER, RANDOLPH, *The world of Flo Ziegfeld*, Elek, London, 1974

CARUSO, DOROTHY, *Enrico Caruso*, T. Werner Laurie, London, 1946

CASTLE, CHARLES, *La Belle Otero*, Michael Joseph, London, 1981

– *The Folies Bergère*, Methuen, London, 1982

CHALIAPIN, see SHALYAPIN

CHARPENTIER, HENRI, *Those Rich and Great Ones*, Gollancz, London, 1935

COHAN, GEORGE M., *Twenty Years on Broadway*, Harper, New York, 1925

CREWE, QUENTIN, *Great Chefs of France*, Mitchell Beazley, London, 1978

DEGHY GUY, *Paradise in the Strand*, Richards Press, London, 1958

DUFF, SIR MOUNTSTUART ELPHINSTONE GRANT, *Victorian Vintage*, Methuen, London, 1930

ESCOFFIER, GEORGES AUGUSTE, *Ma Cuisine*, translated by Vyvyan Holland, Paul Hamlyn, London, 1965

EWEN, DAVID, *Irving Berlin*, Henry Holt & Co, New York, 1950

FANTEL, HANS, *Johann Strauss, father and son*, David & Charles, London, 1971

FERRARO, FILIPPO, *From Candlelight to Flashlight*, Falcon, London, 1952

FILIPPINI, ALESSANDRO, *The Delmonico Cook Book*, Gay & Bird, 1893

FINCK, HENRY THEOPHILUS, *Food and Flavor*, John Lane, London, 1914

– *Massenet and his Operas*, John Lane, London, 1910

– *Richard Strauss*, Little, Brown, Boston, 1917

– *Success in Music*, John Murray, London, 1910

GARDEN, MARY, and BIANCOLLI, L., *Mary Garden's Story*, Michael Joseph, London, 1952

GARTENBERG, EGON, *Vienna, its musical heritage*, Pennsylvania State University Press, 1968

GIGLI, BENIAMINO, *Memoirs*, Cassell, London, 1957

GOTTSCHALK, LOUIS MOREAU, *Notes of a Pianist*, Lippincott, London, 1881

GREENWALL, H. J., *I'm going to Maxim's*, Allan Wingate, London, 1958

HARDING, JAMES, *Gounod*, Allen & Unwin, London, 1973

– *Massenet*, Dent, London, 1970

– *Rossini*, Faber & Faber, London, 1971

HAYWARD, ABRAHAM, *The Art of Dining*, John Murray, London, 1899

HERBODEAU, EUGÈNE ALBERT, *Georges Auguste Escoffier*, Practical Press, London, 1955

HERMAN, JUDITH, and HERMAN, MARGARET SHALETT, *The Cornucopia*, Harper & Row, New York, 1973

HESS, JOHN, *The taste of America*, Penguin, London, 1977

HOWARTH, PATRICK, *When the Riviera Was Ours*, Routledge & Kegan Paul, London, 1977

HUNEKER, JAMES GIBBONS, *Steeplejack*, 2 vols., C. Scribner, New York, 1921

– *Ivory, Apes and Peacocks*, Sagramore Press, New York, 1957

HUROK, SALOMON, *Impresario*, Macdonald, London, 1947

HURST, P. G., *The Age of Jean de Reszke*, Christopher Johnson, London, 1958

HUYSMANS, J. K., *Against the Grain (A Rebours)*, Fortune, London, 1931

JACKSON, STANLEY, *The Savoy*, Frederick Muller, London, 1960

– *Caruso*, W. H. Allen, London, 1972

– *Monsieur Butterfly*, W. H. Allen, London, 1974

JEAFFERSON, J. C., *A Book About the Table*, 2 vols., Hurst & Blackett, London, 1875

JERITZA, MARIA, *Sunlight and Song*, D. Appleton, New York, 1924

JULLIAN, PHILIPPE, *Montmartre*, Phaidon, Oxford, 1977

KEY, PIERRE VAN RENSSELAER, *Enrico Caruso*, Little, Brown, Boston, 1922

LANDON, HOWARD CHANDLER ROBBINS, *Haydn in England, 1791–95*, Thames & Hudson, London, 1976

LIEBLING, ABBOTT JOSEPH, *Between Meals*, Longmans, London, 1962

LEHR, ELIZABETH WHITE DREXEL, *King Lehr and the Gilded Age*, Constable, London, 1935

LEISER, CLARA, *Jean de Reszke and the Great Days of Opera*, Gerald Howe, London, 1933

LONERGAN, WALTER FRANCIS, *Forty Years of Paris*, T. Fisher Unwin, London, 1907

MARCHESI, BLANCHE, *A Singer's Pilgrimage*, Grant Richards, London, 1923

MAXWELL, ELSA, *I married the world*, Heinemann, London, 1955

MORRELL, PARKER, *Diamond Jim*, Hurst & Blackett, London, 1935

MORRIS, HELEN, *Portrait of a Chef. The life of Alexis Soyer*, Cambridge University Press, 1938

NEWMAN, ERNEST, *Life of Richard Wagner*, 4 vols., Cambridge University Press, 1976

NEWTON, IVOR, *At the Piano*, Hamish Hamilton, London, 1966

OFFENBACH, JACQUES, *Orpheus in America*, Hamish Hamilton, London, 1958

PAGE, E. B., and KINGSFORD, P. W., *The Master Chefs*, Arnold, London, 1971

POUGIN, ARTHUR, *Verdi*, Grevel & Co, London, 1887

PUCCINI, GIACOMO, *Letters*, Harrap, London, 1974

RANHOFER, CHARLES, *The Epicurean*, John Willy, Evanston, 1920

RANSOME, ARTHUR, *Bohemia in London*, Chapman & Hall, London, 1907

RECTOR, GEORGE, *The Girl From Rector's*, Heinemann, London, 1927

ROOT, WAVERLEY LEWIS, *The Food of France*, Cassell, London, 1958

SHALYAPIN, FEDOR IVANOVICH, *Pages From My Life*, Harper & Bros, New York, 1927

– *Men and Masks*, Gollancz, London, 1932

SHATTUCK, ROGER, *The Banquet Years*, London, Faber, 1959

SIMON, ANDRÉ LOUIS, *The Art of Good Living*, Constable, London, 1929

– *Tables of Content*, Constable, London, 1933

– *By Request*, Wine & Food Society, London, 1957

SLEZAK, LEO, *Song of Motley*, W. Hodge & Co, London, 1938

SMALLZRIED, KATHLEEN, *The Everlasting Pleasure*, Appleton, New York, 1956

SUTTON, HORACE, *Confessions of a Grand Hotel: the Waldorf-Astoria*, Henry Holt & Co, New York, 1953

TANNAHILL, REAY, *Food in history*, Eyre Methuen, London, 1973

THUDICHUM, J. L. W., *The Spirit of Cookery*, Baillière, London, 1895

TSCHIRKY, OSCAR, *Oscar of the Waldorf Cook Book*, Dover, New York, 1973

TSCHUMI, GABRIEL, *Royal Chef*, William Kimber, London, 1934

WAGNER, WILHELM RICHARD, *My Life*, 2 vols., Constable, London, 1911

WATTS, STEPHEN, *The Ritz*, Bodley Head, London, 1963

WECHSBERG, JOSEPH, *Looking for A Bluebird*, Michael Joseph, London, 1946

– *Sweet and Sour*, Michael Joseph, London, 1949

– *Blue trout and black truffles*, Gollancz, London, 1953

– *Red Plush and Black Velvet*, Weidenfeld, London, 1962

– *Dining at the Pavilion*, Weidenfeld, London, 1963

– *Sounds of Vienna*, Weidenfeld, London, 1968

– *The Waltz Emperors*, Weidenfeld, London, 1973

– *The lost world of the great spas*, Weidenfeld, London, 1979

WILLAN, ANNE, *Great Cooks and Their Recipes*, Elm Tree, London, 1977

WEMYSS, SIR FRANCIS COLCHESTER, *The Pleasures of the Table*, J. Nisbet & Co, London, 1931

VERDI, GIUSEPPE, *Lettere*, 4 vols in Italian, Reale Accademia, Rome, 1935–47

Index

Index

Index